Witch in the Kitchen

me at fourteen. . . *absently stirring something*

on the stove with my nose buried in a book (usual cooking stance).

★ *That's my mother the kitchen goddess on the right.*

Witch in the Kitchen

Magical Cooking for All Seasons

Cait
Johnson

Monoprint Collages by Johanne Renbeck

Destiny Books
Rochester, Vermont

Destiny Books
One Park Street
Rochester, Vermont 05767
www.InnerTraditions.com

Destiny Books is a division of Inner Traditions International

Library of Congress Cataloging-in-Publication Data

Johnson, Cait.
    Witch in the kitchen : magical cooking for all seasons / Cait Johnson.
       p. cm.
    Includes index.
    ISBN 0-89281-980-4 (pbk.)
    1. Cookery. 2. Cookery—Religious aspects. I. Title.
  TX714 .J62 2001
  641.5—dc21

                                                          2001003395

Printed and bound in the United States

10 9 8 7 6 5 4 3 2 1

Text design by Cindy Sutherland

This book was typeset in Goudy with Apple Chancery as the display typeface

Contents

part 3: winter

part 4: spring

part 5: summer

Acknowledgments

I *offer my devotion* to the personal pantheon of Great Ones who oversaw the original cookbook project, were involved with this new, winged version, and who generally guide and shape my life: Artemis of Ephesus, Brigid, Cailleach, the Dagda, Demeter, Durga, Hecate, Kali, Lilith, Persephone, Sheela, and especially the Shaman of Wands, Son of Wands, and Queen of Discs.

Great gratitude to my spirit-sister, author Elizabeth Cunningham. Her powerful words have infused *Witch in the Kitchen* with her own special brand of wisdom and humor, and her presence in my life fills me with abundance.

My deep thanks to Maura D. Shaw, who is sometimes my coauthor and always a fine writer and soul-friend. Her vision was instrumental in birthing the first incarnation of this book.

This project was inspired, supported, and sometimes transformed by my generous friends: hugs and thanks to Santha Cooke, Nadine Daugherty, Elaine Fletcher, Karen Holtslag, Kerri Karvetski, Ashling Kelly, Farah Shaw Kelsey, Jessica Kemper, Laurel Kerr, Richard Kramer, Pangea Jaeger, Donnalynne Lefever, Nina Lewis, Rhianna Mirabello, Anne Nightingale, Nancy Rowe, Regina Seigel, Sandy Sklar, and Raven Wild. I feel so very fortunate to be surrounded by their loving enthusiasm.

Many thanks to my son, Reid, for his willingness to try new things and for his sometimes devastating honesty after he has! His directness, humor, and love of sushi continue to amaze me. My parents are a fine source of encouragement: It helps to be believed in. And my most heartfelt gratitude to my sweetheart, Joe Bartusis, who heals me with his tenderness and fills our kitchen with laughter and our bellies with wonderful food.

Blessings on my marvelous editor, Elaine Sanborn. She delighted me throughout the prepublication process with recipes, gardening bulletins, and a shared love of animals and theater performance. All this, keen judgment, and sensitivity, too— what bliss! Also my thanks to Susan Millen, artist and dear friend, who created the absolutely delicious cover. And honor to Johanne Renbeck, for the spirit and depth of her monoprint collages that add such magic to the four seasons of this book.

Preface

$\mathcal{M}$any years ago, my mother sent me a knickknack called a kitchen witch—a calico-skirted figure glued to a twig broomstick, with a benign if stereotypical nose-meets-chin sort of face—with the suggestion that I hang it over my kitchen cabinets. The manufacturer's tag assured me that this kitchen witch was a traditional source of good luck. I found it both amusing and touching to think of ordinary women all over the country hanging these little magical icons over their stoves and cupboards without knowing that there were real kitchen witches who really did make magic. Just a few years before my mother sent me that little good-luck figure, I had learned not only that real witches existed, but also that the term *kitchen witch* refers to pagans who practice informally, with the tools at hand and a deep appreciation for the sacred in the everyday. With a sense of having finally come home, I embraced this group as my own.

Now I have come to realize that there are many ways of being a kitchen witch. Your grandmothers and great-grandmothers probably knew a few of them, since many of our foremothers were Wise Ones who celebrated the magic in food, in cooking, and in kitchens, those home-hearts where family and friends are nurtured. Today we may not be used to thinking of our kitchens as magical places, but they are. Cooking was once considered a sacred act. After all, the cauldron and the stewpot are clearly related, and making a meal from a recipe is akin to casting a spell. Ingredients are gathered with intention, specific actions are performed in a certain order with a desired outcome in mind, and then—voilà!—the magic is served up. And there is a very potent magic available to us as we cook. We can do so with the conscious and loving intention that our food will connect us joyfully to the great Earth and her seasons, deeply nourishing us all.

This book is a revised and updated version of *Cooking Like a Goddess*, which was written several years ago when the word *witch* was still a bit incendiary for the general reading audience. Now, joyously out of the broom closet and with the addition of new spells and magical poetry, *Witch in the Kitchen* has emerged with wings to match the Wiccan roots that were always there.

Witches have a special relationship with food; we understand its importance in the sacred scheme of things. I have always deeply appreciated the fact that *SageWoman* magazine, that ally and guide for so many witches, includes recipes right along with its articles, poems, and rituals. *The Beltane Papers*, too, gives food its magical due. Food is the Goddess, and enjoying her is part of the whole ritual experience. My sisters in Full Moon groups always brought platters and bowls heaped with homemade goodies to be shared in the circle. One particularly memorable autumn moon included the eating of a special pie with our hands only—no utensils! A sticky and delicious time was had by all, and I came to realize that this sense of holy fun, of sacred sensuality, is at the root of all my work.

Like so many of you, I have always been a witch. From earliest childhood, I made seasonal altars, danced with green spirits under the trees, and devoted my life to awareness of the magic in all things. But twenty-seven years had passed before I met my first Wiccan priestess and learned that there was an actual Goddess Path. At first performing by-the-book rituals, making up complicated spells, and delving into tarot and the use of other divination tools made up the backbone of my spiritual practice. Spells, especially, gave me a feeling of empowerment: I could direct my will to change things—no more suffering in silence! Now, twenty-or-so years later my way of dancing with Wicca has slowly transformed. I facilitate simple Wheel of the Year celebrations that focus less on formal ceremony and more on joyful community. When I engage in spirit-centered activities the intent is more often to open myself, to embrace and accept the potential for growth in what is, rather than to change things to suit my desires. My relationship with tarot has deepened into a counseling practice that helps people live more authentically, encouraging them to truly embody the needs of their souls. And the magic of the Goddess continues to guide and inspire me.

Witch in the Kitchen is my personal testimonial to the transformative power of cooking and eating with spirit awareness. In the past two years my life has changed utterly. As of this writing, I am living with a loving, gentle man who cooks—and cooks better than I do! My heart is filled with a kind of stunned gratitude. So I offer this book with love to everyone who longs to live in celebration of the divine Mystery, in deep and delicious relationship with magic. May we all become the people our souls long to be, for the good of all. So mote it be.

Introduction

All living things eat and are eaten. It's cooking that makes us human.
—**Elizabeth Cunningham**

This book is for all of us who would like cooking and eating to be more magical and deeply soul satisfying. If you have ever felt hungry after you've just eaten, if you long to recover the ancient sense that your hearth is sacred, if you want to feel more connected to the Earth and to your own inner Wild One, or if you simply need some inspiration in the kitchen, then *Witch in the Kitchen* is for you.

Side by side with the recipes here are rituals, spells, meditations, playful exercises—even decorating ideas—that deepen our relationship to food and to the Earth. We are all inextricably connected to our mother planet and to the food she gives us, but many of us have forgotten that the connection is a sacred one. When we remember, then food may become the key to sacred experience. Our bodies will open the door and show us the way through. And the entire process can be great, nourishing fun.

So welcome to the world of *Witch in the Kitchen*, a world presided over by loving seasonal goddesses who want nothing better than to share their gifts with us. Prepare to dance with them as they sing their songs and show us how to fully embody and appreciate each phase of the yearly cycle.

Together, we will explore the idea of cooking as a nourishing spiritual practice. This doesn't mean that we will need to spend more time cooking or that the meals we prepare will become more elaborate (in fact, they often become much simpler). Instead, exploring the sacredness of cooking means cooking with mindful awareness, with deeply felt pleasure and playful creativity, using foods that reflect the changing energies of the seasons, that are in harmony with the cycles of the Earth and those of your own body. When we cook with a sense of magic and mindfulness, we can all be witches in the kitchen.

The recipes in this book are simple and comforting. Out of a mouthwatering multitude of possibilities, I chose these particular foods because they seem to typify each season, to be filled with those special flavors, colors, and textures. I relied upon my own tastes and intuition for inspiration, and I encourage you to do the same. If, for example, a particular food summons up springlike feelings in you but I didn't include it in the Spring section, by all means go ahead and cook it—with gusto—in spring! This book is about trusting your longings and honoring who you are; the recipes are designed to allow plenty of creative individual variation.

It does our hearts good (both literally and figuratively, I think) to eat what Mahatma Gandhi called "innocent food," food that does not cause suffering to any living creature. The fact that there are many people starving on this planet of ours makes eating low on the food chain a humane priority. And there is a special sense of blessing, one that can be felt in every cell of our bodies, when we eat foods that come directly from our Mother Earth. And so these recipes are vegetarian, not in any spirit of self-denial, but rather in the spirit of loving connection to the most vibrant and healthful energies of the Earth.

How we eat—our frame of mind and heart—may be just as important as what we eat. We can all name relatives or friends who drink like fish, smoke, eat terrible things, and are eighty years old and still going strong. Likewise, many of us are busy doing all the right things—fretting over proper food combinations, cutting out anything remotely "bad" or dangerous (no caffeine, no alcohol), agonizing over every gram of fat, and all the rest of it—and we're not exactly glowing with health.

Perhaps the key is to relax, to connect with the earth and the food it gives us, and to live joyously. *Witch in the Kitchen* is designed to help us live in a more joyful and connected way. And although there are no guarantees that joyful and connected living will prolong your life, it will certainly make life a pleasure while you live it.

One thing *Witch in the Kitchen* is not designed to give you is guilt. Even though I love to cook, cooking is not my only spiritual practice; I don't spend all day, every day, in the kitchen fixing fancy meals for my family. I would often rather be making clay goddesses or reading or taking a walk in the woods or writing than cooking (in fact, I scorched one of the soups I was testing for this book because I got busy at the laptop and lost track of time). And I must confess that I take shortcuts when I need to; all-natural pilafs from a box, for instance, make a pretty consistent appearance on our table.

It may be that your life is too hectic to allow time for trying any of the rituals, spells, meditations, or ideas. If that's so, don't worry; simply reading them will help. (Thousands of us curl up in bed with a good cookbook whenever we need comfort. Cookbooks often work even better than mysteries or escapist fantasies to give us what we need. And we don't necessarily cook the recipes we read about, either.)

The truth is we are all very busy doing other things; food preparation isn't always at the top of our list of priorities. What really matters is not how much or how often we cook, but how deeply we pay attention when we do the cooking we do. Many of us are used to thinking that fixing a meal is something to rush through so we can get to the more important stuff. When we realize that cooking is itself an important—even sacred—act, perhaps we will no longer resent the time we spend in the kitchen. Perhaps we can be authentic, juicy, and deeply alive both in and out of the kitchen.

Witch in the Kitchen invites us to interact with our food in playful and magical ways, to love our kitchens, our bodies, and our planet. When we welcome the goddesses of the seasons into our hearts, we will see that the magical world of this book is the real world that has surrounded and sustained us since the beginning of time. We will be priestesses in our kitchens, we will be cooking (and eating) like goddesses—and we will have come home.

Making Your Kitchen a Sacred Space

If you have mixed feelings about your kitchen, you are not alone. Our attitudes toward kitchens and cooking are often weighted with lots of baggage, at least some of which is a legacy from our mothers, who often had pretty mixed feelings themselves. For many of our mothers, boxed and frozen foods were the saviors that liberated them from domestic tyranny and bought them a little free time; we may have grown up never knowing that food could taste alive. Others had moms who liked to do things the traditional way. Those meals probably tasted great, but we may have been thinking, as we chewed, "*I am never going to spend five hours laboring over a meal that will get wolfed down in fifteen minutes. No such slavery for me, thank you!*"

For some of us, even warm and cozy images of the kitchen are inextricably entwined with images, just as strong, of patriarchal oppression: We know that there were generations of women who had no other arena for their abilities, no other outlet for their talents. With phrases like "Barefoot, pregnant, and in the kitchen" echoing in our heads, it's easy to see how kitchens can become symbols of frustration, of gifts denied. And those of us who truly love to cook may catch ourselves wondering, "Am I somehow not liberated? Is it politically incorrect to like hanging out in the kitchen? Should I be pacing a boardroom instead?"

Kitchens are often synonymous with some very complex issues. For instance, they automatically seem to bring up our deep-seated attitudes about sexual equality. Was your childhood kitchen solely your mother's domain? If it was, did your mom resent her kitchen responsibilities, or did she revel in her role as Kitchen Queen? Where did your dad fit in? Where did you? If you're in a relationship, how does your significant other fit into your kitchen scenario? Some of us have partners who never set foot in the kitchen.

Others have partners who do all, or at least the majority, of the cooking. What are the kitchen dynamics in your home? How do you feel about them?

The central truth—whether we're partnered or solo, on a high-powered career track, staying at home with our children, or somewhere in between—is that we all have to spend some time in the kitchen. We all have to eat. Some of us have to feed other people besides ourselves. And sadly, for many of us kitchens are just rooms where we have to spend too much time, places of tedious and soulless drudgery. It's no wonder that many of us feel tired, turned off, and bored as soon as we walk into them. Somehow, our culture has stolen the spirit from cooking, and from food. It is perhaps no coincidence that eating disorders are so prevalent: our very souls are hungry.

But what if we could restore a sense of magic, joy, and sacredness to the whole complex package of cooking and eating and kitchens? Imagine creating a kitchen that fills you with a sense of your own magical power—whether you spend three minutes a day cooking in it or three hours. Imagine finding a way home to your ancient birthright of soul nourishment and deep pleasure in food. Imagine reveling in the spell of each season as you bring its special ingredients to life. Imagine cooking like a witch in the kitchen.

This chapter offers a lively and empowering antidote to the cultural deadness surrounding kitchens, cooking, and food. In it, we are invited to create kitchens that are vivid expressions of our wild spirits, that resonate with our inner selves—kitchens where we can begin to feel deeply at home. By restoring a sense of the sacred and magical to cooking and eating, we nourish our deep inner hunger, a hunger for connectedness and meaning. We can begin to create a concept of sacredness that embraces the everyday, that includes the playful and the spontaneous in its expression.

For all of us with mixed and complex feelings about kitchens and food, it can help to know that there is a tradition—newly rediscovered by witches everywhere—called the Goddess Way or the Pagan Path, where food is considered holy, the body of our sacred Mother Earth, a loving gift to her children. Our culture may have forgotten this path, but our ancestors knew it; indigenous peoples have always known it. It is an

Earth-centered way, meaning that it is grounded in loving respect for the planet. It is an ancient way, but it is reemerging today to remind us of our ancient goddess heritage. According to the Goddess Way or Pagan Path, food can be our spiritual guide, a guide that leads us to direct experience of the numinous, the Divine. Food is sacred. Our kitchens can be sacred, too.

Our culture considers cooking a chore; we are encouraged to get it over with as quickly as possible. But it may help us to remember that cooking was once a magical act. Cooks were priestesses who wielded the power of fire, transforming raw ingredients into nourishment for themselves and their families. The act of cooking linked women with the Goddess, the Great Nurturer. Now we can reclaim our power and joy in cooking, not because it is the only thing we are allowed to do, but because it is a sacred act and we are just the sacred folks to do it. We can reclaim the importance of the things women have always done—caretaking, teaching, relating, creating, mothering—because they have kept humanity alive despite our culture's message that only warfare, gaining power over others, consumerism, and competition are important.

Our culture may have taught us that we are widely separated by our differences—racial, religious, sexual, economic. But the need for food gives all of us a common bond. And the fact that we are all inhabitants of this planet gives us another. Many of us are busy reenvisioning and remaking our culture in a healthier, more life-affirming mold. We want to imagine a culture where all of us are empowered to nurture each other and ourselves. It can all start in the kitchen.

The following sections offer ideas for making your kitchen a place where magic can happen, a place that feels deeply right to you, an evocation of your unique and powerful spirit. At this point, many of you may be thinking, "Look, I hardly have the time or energy to throw a frozen burrito in the microwave. Now I'm supposed to redecorate my kitchen? Are you kidding?"

The good news is that making your kitchen sacred is a process. Take it at the pace that feels right to you. Do only the things that feel fun. And use these ideas as inspiration for your own flights of spirit-fancy—there aren't any rules here except to follow your inclinations, listen to your heart. The strange and wonderful paradox here is that the more you make time to do, the more energy you'll have. Part of our deep spiritual exhaustion stems from the hours and hours we spend doing things that don't feed our spirit. Playing with magic in the kitchen will nourish and revive you.

Our ancestors knew the pleasure of being firmly rooted in their kitchens *and* in their magic. Sadly, our culture is a rootless one—as my friend the novelist Elizabeth Cunningham says, most of us are walking around like cut flowers. Here, then, are some ideas and inspiration for putting down roots in the kitchen, making it a place where your goddess-self will feel deeply and joyously at home.

Putting Down Roots

*T*he *secret to making our kitchens sacred places* is to connect: connect with inner self, connect with Deeper Power, connect with the living energies of the foods we cook. It is through the act of connection that we put down spirit-roots that draw up nourishment from the deep place to feed our hungry souls. And our greatest allies when it comes to this process of connecting and putting down roots are our senses.

Many of us have been taught that our bodies are lowly, even shameful, certainly inferior to the white light of Spirit, that only our minds are to be trusted—never our senses. Now many of us are realizing that this may not be the healthiest attitude to take. Witches know that our bodies are wise beyond our imagining; they give us cues to communicate that wisdom. Our bodies are, in fact, sacred and should be treated as sacred. Is it any wonder that the kitchen, so clearly tied to the needs of the body, should have been considered a lowly and inferior place for so long?

As we reclaim the sanctity of the body, we reclaim the sacredness of the kitchen. Trusting our senses is a first step. Our bodies need to be not only at ease, but also pleased in the kitchen. We can't put down roots if the very sight, feel, and smell of the place make us tense and unhappy. So first we need to take a good look at the materials that were used to make our kitchens. Natural ones—wood, tile, brick—seem to encourage rooting, but materials that were man-made (the term is used advisedly) do not.

So what do you do if yours is an artificial kitchen? Do you have to rip out everything and replace it with natural pine and earthy tile? Fortunately, no (unless you've been searching for a project that would take lots of money and time). Instead, you could do what a friend did when she moved into her new home and was confronted with the Kitchen from the Chemical Lab: She put rag rugs over the linoleum, painted spirals and suns on the Formica cabinets, and replaced the Formica-topped built-in table with an old pine one. If you can't renovate, redecorate! Let's hope the surfaces you see and touch most often will end up being pleasing to you.

Cleaning

A tidy kitchen is certainly not a prerequisite for sacred cooking—our inner Wild One has absolutely nothing against an exuberant mess. But a kitchen that smells weird or feels nasty can make your spirit cringe.

If you've been putting off the odious task of cleaning, you can make the process a more spirit-connected one in several ways:

1. Sing a special song as you clean. If you know a goddess song, great. If not, make up something. Repeating even the simplest of tunes (with or without rhyming words) can help you to relax, open, deepen. You don't have to sound like a "professional"— don't judge yourself, just have fun with it.

2. Clean barefoot. (Or naked.) This changes one's perspective, somehow. As you work, visualize rootlets growing from the soles of your feet, going down through your (clean) floor into the Earth.

3. Make yourself a cleaner's crown out of ribbon or paper or ivy or anything that strikes your fancy. After all, you deserve a crown for all the work you do. Make up a silly name for yourself. If you're a warrior-type, you could be Spic 'n' Spanna, Fighter of Grime; make up stories about your battles and adventures. Or become Our Lady of Perpetual Mopping; see yourself as a healer and soother, a sort of Mother Teresa of the kitchen. Your crown would be more of a halo. Maybe you'd be happy as the Wise One of the Woods, wreathed with wild grapevine, breasts painted with magical symbols (real or imagined). Find a character that suits you.

4. Nothing discourages rooting like toxic and carcinogenic chemicals. If your cleaning products are filled with them, you can bet your inner self knows it—and it probably isn't happy. There are many wonderful books available today that tell how to make safe, effective household cleaners from simple and natural ingredients (see the Suggested Reading section for titles). Or take a trip to your nearest natural foods store and try some of the earth-friendly products you'll find there. You'll be doing yourself, your family, and the environment a favor—and you'll feel a healthy difference in your kitchen. Imagine wiping away the grease with a liquid made of deliciously scented citrus peels instead of harsh chemicals. Or scouring the sink with fresh lemon and baking soda rather than something that smells like a public swimming pool. What you choose to use can really make a difference. Try paper towels made from non-chlorine-bleached recycled paper, or switch to washable cloths. When you grocery-shop, bring along a string bag or a sturdy canvas one. Compost your kitchen scraps, rather than just throwing them away. Actually, composting can become a satisfying part of our daily spiritual practice. Here is a Compost Prayer from my friend Pangea. She repeats it every time she takes the kitchen-scrap crock outside to empty it onto her compost heap.

From the earth you came—
Your seed did grow,
Nourishing all of me, body and soul,
An eternal cycle,
A graceful flow—
And now, back into the earth you go.
Blessed be, Mother Earth. Thank you.

Even small, everyday choices like these can show that we care about the planet. After all, when we put down roots, we want the earth we root in to be healthy and safe.

5. Add a strong herbal tea to your cleaning water. The sweet scent and good vibes will go a long way toward making your kitchen feel connected to Deep Power. Just boil a couple of cups of water and throw in a handful of herbs, steep for several minutes, and then strain the tea into your cleaning bucket.

Here are some traditional herb correspondences; choose one or more according to your desire. We don't usually think of things like sea salt and basil and apples as magical, but our witchy ancestors knew they were. It is a wonderful affirmation of the magic in the ordinary to use kitchen-cupboard ingredients consciously in this way. And that, after all, is part of what being a kitchen witch is all about.

angelica: Blessings, protection, purification. Those of you who are fascinated by angels will like this one; think of it as inviting angels into your home.

apples: Food of the Goddess; love. Simply add a few pieces of fresh or dried apple to your boiling water (but not too much or you'll end up with a sticky kitchen).

basil: Love, fidelity, wealth, protection. A nice all-purpose herb with a luscious summery scent reminiscent of mouthwatering pesto.

chamomile: Serenity and calm; purification. Smells like a blend of apples and new-mown hay. While you're at it, make yourself a cup of tea to drink after you've finished cleaning; it's very relaxing.

cinnamon: Happy home, safety, healing, protection. The primal home-and-hearth spice. Use pieces of cinnamon stick for your brew (the powdered kind will turn into a gelatinous glop in the bowl).

clove: Purification; promotes love and spirituality. Try it with cinnamon—delicious!

eucalyptus: Health; protection. Slightly medicinal, but warm and fresh.

evergreen: Health, purification, vitality. Different types have different scents, so experiment. If you have pine, cedar, or juniper growing nearby, a few sprigs placed in boiling water will add green freshness to the brew.

fennel: Protection, healing. Its licorice scent has a quality, reminiscent of childhood, that's very appealing.

lavender: Love, friendship, peace, happiness, protection. Such a sweet, relaxing, and calm-inducing scent—and it's also an antidepressant.

lemon peel (fresh or dried): Purification. It's no accident that so many cleaning products are lemon-scented; lemon smells fresh and uplifting and cleanses away negativity.

marjoram: Love, protection. Another antidepressant. Some of us sprinkle a little of this dried herb in the corners of every room in the house (why stop with the kitchen?) to promote love and safety.

peppermint: Purification, healing, soothing. A wonderfully relaxing and refreshing scent.

rosemary: Cleansing and protection; clears negativity; encourages clear thinking. You may find that a rosemary-smelling kitchen is one where you have to consult the recipe less often because you'll find yourself remembering what it says!

sage: Purification, wisdom. It's no coincidence that the word for *wise one* is the same as the herb's name. A traditional ingredient of many Native American smudge bundles, a strong sage tea will make your kitchen feel safe and cleared of negativity.

St. Joan's (or John's) Wort: Health, happiness, love, protection. An all-purpose herb. It doesn't really have a scent, but a few drops of tincture—or a few blossoms strewn in the wash water—give many benefits. Consult a good weed identification book to see if there is any growing near you, or see Supplies to order the tincture.

sea salt: Traditional for purification and protection. If you've been feeling vulnerable or weird and you have time to add only one ingredient to your water, this could be it.

vanilla: Love, happiness. A piece of the bean or a few drops of extract will make your kitchen smell and feel delicious.

If you're stressed for time or low on ingredients, try the herbal tea bag shortcut. There are many varieties available at the supermarket with nice combinations of ingredients already premixed for you. For instance, Celestial Seasonings makes a fragrant cinnamon-apple blend, perfect for happy-home and goddess-centered energies. If it's serenity in the kitchen that you want, try one of the many stress-reducing or relaxing blends available. Just boil a few cups of water, add a couple of bags, steep, and strain as usual.

Or use a few drops of essential oil instead of either tea bags or herbs. Consult a good book on aromatherapy to see which scents would be most beneficial for you and your family.

6. After you've vanquished the worst of the grime, clear the atmosphere by lighting a sweetgrass braid or sage-based smudge bundle and walk around the room, letting the smoke waft into every corner (let some smoke waft into the cupboards, too). Or light a stick or cone of your favorite incense. You want your kitchen to smell good to your inner self.

7. You may surprise yourself and really get into the cleaning process. If you do (and if you have some more time), you may enjoy clearing out and beautifully organizing your cupboards. Virgo-type friends report that every time they open a tidied cupboard, the sight of neatly arranged cans and jars—or cups and plates—gives them a rush of serenity and well-being. Even non-Virgos can enjoy this.

8. Take some special time in your now clean kitchen, simply being, doing nothing. You will be amazed at how soothing this can be. Make yourself a cup of tea and just sit and drink it. Slowly. Quietly. Listen to the hum of your refrigerator. Smell the incense or smudge or herbs that you used. Feel the shape of the chair under your seat, the firmness of the floor under your feet. You are enspiriting your kitchen—now you can allow yourself to feel welcomed by that spirit, which you are helping to create.

The Power Place

One of the most important first steps in making your kitchen sacred is to create a place of nurturance for yourself there. We deserve to have a special spot where we can relax, close our eyes and meditate, daydream, or simply think about food in peace. Tuning in to your inner self and feeling empowered are more difficult when your muscles are tensed. You are the goddess of your kitchen: You deserve to be comfortable.

All you really need is a special, cozy chair—one that everyone in your home recognizes as yours. Every time you sit in it, you will remember that you are doing sacred work when you cook, and you will remember that comfort was once the special gift of the kitchen.

Even though many of our modern kitchens are sleek, almost chilly places, something in our bones remembers when kitchens were snug. Deep inside us, we remember the magical glow from a cave-fire. Outside its bright circle of protection were all our fears—hungry wild beasts, killing cold, shapeless terrors that waited in the dark. But inside the golden circle we were safe. Kitchens—places where the hearth fires burn—mean safety, warmth, peace. For centuries, the kitchen was virtually the only comfortable room in the house. Before central heating, its roaring fires and ovens kept out the chill when the world was blanketed with snow. The kitchen became a natural gathering place, with special seats built near the fireplace where one could rest and be at ease, warm, and comfortable.

Hold that image of warmth and comfort in your mind while you look around your kitchen. Is the seating soft and inviting? Is there any seating at all? If you live in a tiny city apartment, you may not even have room for a chair. In this case, you can design a movable cushioned space for yourself on the floor; you can move the cushion when you need to open the oven door.

If you do have space for a table and chairs, really notice how they feel. Kitchen chairs are often hard and bumpy. If your chair makes your seat and spirit sore, consider haunting yard sales and thrift shops until you find a rounder, softer, or more cushioned alternative. An acquaintance flouted convention recently and bought herself a lush, forties-style brocaded armchair from the Salvation Army for her kitchen corner. Now she can curl up in the lap of luxury, and read cookbooks (or murder mysteries). She reports that it has changed the way she feels about her kitchen forever. Having a place to plop down and relax while the stew is bubbling or the bread is baking feels very soothing to the soul.

We create inviting kitchens not only for ourselves, but also for our families. Most of us have a real longing to share our emerging sense of deep nourishment with the people we love. But even though we want to share our kitchens with loved ones, it is important for us to stake out this special chair or spot for ourselves alone. Accessing our inner power is much easier when we have a place from which to access it. A Power Place becomes an important part of our conscious effort to reclaim the role of Kitchen Priestess, freeing us from the martyrdom and domestic slavery so long associated with kitchen work. And children who see their parent consciously modeling this claiming of kitchen power will have an easier time growing into their own some day.

So claim your spot, and fill your kitchen with textures and colors that make you feel nourished and safe. When we make the kitchen a serene and comfortable place, we create a heart of safety in a very unsafe world. It is what women have done for eons: made nests of nurturance and peace for their families. We need those nests more than ever now.

Convenience

Most of us organize our kitchens the way our mothers organized theirs; after all, it's what we grew up with, what we're used to. But it is often worth some time and thought to see if a few changes would make your kitchen feel more like you, more appropriate for who you are. Why not put your boxes of tea bags in the same cabinet as the mugs and cups? Then you'd have to open only one door to make a cup of tea. Why not devote an entire cupboard to herbs and spices if you want to? Or if you paint, why not set aside a shelf for your supplies? Or clear a space on the table for the laptop, if you're a writer? It's wonderfully empowering to free ourselves from compartmentalized thinking and living. Ask yourself, "Why not?" if you want to do something a little different. There's no reason that we can't make room in the kitchen for the activities we love most deeply. And as we give some deep attention to the way we want to live our lives, throwing out any arbitrary rules along the way, we just may find that we have made our lives a seamless and magical whole. What a wonderful healing that would be!

Allies in the Kitchen

Most of us use gadgets, utensils, and appliances when we cook. There are elaborate electronic ones, ranging from fancy food processors, cappuccino machines, dishwashers, microwaves, and breadmakers to the more ubiquitous refrigerators and blenders. Even the low-tech cook usually has a toaster or an electric handheld beater. Not everybody has egg separators or apple corers, but we all use knives, spatulas, and spoons. And a kitchen isn't a kitchen without an oven and a stove.

Most of us make use of these kitchen allies every day—and a sudden power failure has shown more than a few of us how dependent on the electric ones we are. But for many of us, appliances can feel a little alien. We may find ourselves thinking, "I don't know how the heck it works, so it must be dangerous." And even the most technologically dauntless among us have been known to curse a faulty appliance when things go wrong. When we're not secretly fearing or actively despising our appliances, we remain somehow aloof and detached from them—after all, they're just hunks of metal and plastic from the store. But this distancing is not conducive to rooting. Our ancestors made all of their kitchen utensils lovingly by hand; their tools were rich with spirit-value. So how can we create an aura of warmth and friendliness around the tools we use? The answer is by personalizing them.

Try imagining our appliances as helpful genies who gladly share space in our kitchens in order to do our bidding—the bidding of the Kitchen Witch. Take some time to really look at them, their colors, their shapes. By simply observing them, we can discover (or invent) their personalities. A battered old automatic dishwasher, for instance, could be seen as a rounded, genial type, dowdy but capable—and very different from the assertive, breezy new toaster with its slick, shiny finish. We may choose to honor these newly discovered personalities by naming our appliances, just as many of us name our cars. ("I'll call you back—Dante's preheated; I've got to put the muffins in"; "We'll have clean glasses in a minute—Ethel's nearly finished her dry cycle"; "Could you put the leftovers on Nanook's top shelf, behind the milk?")

If that's just not your style, you could try a different approach, which involves making your own personal and individual mark on the tools you use. Try decorating your appliances and utensils, either subtly or not so subtly, depending on your preference. Children's stickers and lick-and-stick stamps are quick ways to do this; the more artistically inclined may want to hand-paint or stencil something personally significant—a totem animal, a favorite flower or fruit, a special symbol. The handles of your wooden tools may be carved; plastic ones may be painted.

Touching a drop of your favorite essential oil to your major appliances is another way to mark them, much as a cat rubs its chin glands on things to mark territory or special preference. Or if you feel your inner Wild One stirring, you could use your own saliva to celebrate your bond with your kitchen allies!

The simple act of consciously choosing to buy only things that are pleasing to your eye and to your touch is another way to give spirit to your utensils: The antique egg-beater that holds a mysterious appeal for you will make the act of whipping cream with it a real pleasure, even though it takes longer than with a fancy electric gadget. You may also notice that a kitchen gift from a special friend makes you feel warm and happy every time you take it out of the drawer. Certainly, the plates and bowls, cups, glasses, and eating utensils you use should be pleasing to you. If they're not, consider having a swap with friends; you may have just what the other wants or needs. If you have pottery skills and access to clay and a kiln, you could make a simple set of dinnerware yourself, as one friend's husband did. Or you could collect plates and bowls hand-thrown by your favorite potter, piece by piece, as you can afford them. Thrift shops and yard sales often yield magical treasures, like the tiny brass teaspoons, each with a different mythical beast on the handle, that were a garage-sale gift from my partner, and my favorite Staffordshire plate painted with autumnal grapes and roses, bought for a dollar at the Salvation Army.

But the simplest method of connecting with the things in your kitchen involves nothing more complicated than using these tools with consciousness. Become aware of their smoothness, their shape, the way they move or work, the noises they make. Hum along with your dishwasher, or hold your hands next to a hot oven and feel the power of its flame. When you push a button or pick a setting, explore your own power to choose, to do, to make.

Creativity

Each of the four seasonal sections in this book includes many ideas for decorating your kitchen creatively and in harmony with the Earth. The most important thing will be to trust your sense of what is *right for you.*

Part of owning our witch power is banishing the "shoulds" and "shouldn'ts" from our kitchens. Who says you shouldn't hang a phalanx of winged goddesses over the sink? Who says you shouldn't hand-paint bright suns and pentacles on the backsplash behind the countertops or on the fridge if you want to? Who says you have to paint anything at all if you really like things bare? It's your kitchen. (If you are a renter with a longing for painted decoration and the owner disapproves, you could explore the ways in which double-stick tape can be used to temporarily apply unusual shapes and colors to your appliances and cupboards.)

This book is based on creativity: trusting our inner self, really taking time to savor and experience food, allowing our inclinations and the nature of the ingredients themselves to determine what we cook. When our kitchen becomes the reflection of a creative relationship with the inner self, we affirm creativity in every aspect of our lives.

Community

Kitchens can be the perfect place to party. Many of us have often noted that the kitchen is where guests tend to congregate anyway, whether or not you want them to. You may want to throw a kitchen-warming party in honor of your newly consecrated cooking space—invite your closest friends and family for a potluck or, better yet, have a Community Cook, to which everybody brings raw ingredients. The cooking then becomes a group effort. (Depending on the size of your kitchen and the amount of wine consumed, this can be a fairly hilarious process.)

When we invite the people we love to celebrate our sacred kitchen with us, we set the seal of that love on our efforts, and we invest the room with happy memories and good energy. And we also create a vital sense of community based on the values of the sacred kitchen. What a lovely, lively way to spread the word!

The Kitchen Altar

Many cultures still make a place in their kitchens to honor Greater Power. We can, too. A kitchen altar makes a vital, visual connection between you and your cooking activities and this power, whatever you conceive it to be. If the oven and stove, as modern equivalents of the hearth fire, are the heart of the house, this altar will be the soul. Every time you see it, you will be reminded that what you do is vitally important. It will remind you that your kitchen is a sacred place. It will help you remember that your ability to nourish yourself and your loved ones connects you with the Great Mother, the Nourisher, the spirit of loving and compassionate care.

And the kitchen altar is meant to be a joyous and playful expression of your wild spirit—creating it is great fun! Whenever we consciously allow our inner self to come out and play, a deep satisfaction results from feeding our spirits and nurturing our souls. While your altar will be unique because each one of us is so different, it is also comforting to know that it connects you to many, many other people with unique altars of their own.

Here, then, are some guidelines to help you get started. You could also check out some books from your local library or bookstore—pictures of altars from different countries will be sure to inspire you (see Russia's gilded kitchen icons, the terra-cotta niches of Mexico, or any of the powerful elemental altars found in many African countries). Search out the cultures that most closely match your own heritage, if you like. Or wing it and invent your own.

Kitchen Goddesses

It is very ancient and powerful magic to have a goddess figure in your home. Some of the earliest human artifacts ever discovered include many domestic goddess statues. When we create an altar and house a goddess there, we are making a satisfying link with our earliest ancestors. Many of us have found that having a female figure in this place of honor just feels deeply right. (It's difficult even to picture any of the great male religious figures bent over a cooking pot, stirring away.) Although goddess worship was officially squelched for centuries, scores of kitchen deities from cultures around the globe prove you just can't keep a good goddess down.

Today, we can find or create special kitchen goddesses to be the focus for our altars. In fact, a good first step in creating your altar is choosing the goddess you wish to honor with it. Your kitchen altar becomes this deity's home, as well as a place to honor who *you* are and what *you* do.

When you make a kitchen altar, you begin a special, personal, and very intimate relationship with your kitchen goddess. In some ways, the two of you will echo each other; it is important to choose a goddess that embodies traits and values that you desire or with which you can identify. There are several books in the Suggested Reading section that will help you pick one who is right for you. Or you could invent or re-create a goddess especially for your kitchen.

Once you've decided on your goddess, you may purchase a likeness of her—there are several wonderful sources for reproductions of ancient figures (see Supplies)—or you can make your own with clay or Sculpey or papier-mâché or improvise something magical with twigs, weeds, or fabric.

If three-dimensional figures aren't your style (or you aren't able to find one that you like), try cutting out a photo or painting and gluing it onto cardboard. You can create a textured border around this flat surface with glue and trim, or with tendrils of ivy or some other potted houseplant.

The expression on your goddess's face is very important; you'll find that it can affect your cooking mood. A picture of mild-faced Hestia, eyes peacefully focused on the hearth fire, will give you one feeling; Kali, with her necklace of skulls, fierce scowl, and tongue hanging out, will give you quite another. And there is certainly no law against having more than one kitchen goddess. They can be rotated to suit the season or your mood—each could take her turn vacationing, soaking up some sun in the backyard, while someone else takes her turn on the altar.

And we certainly don't need to exclude males here. One friend is perfectly happy with her (male) kitchen dragon, while another tells me that her kitchen goddess has a consort from Trinidad—"And who knows what they get up to when we're not looking?" If you want to have a male kitchen deity, great! (Ironically, with all of my own personal emphasis on the Goddess, it was a male—the Son of Wands from the Motherpeace Tarot deck—who appeared in a tarot session and encouraged me to continue this cookbook project.)

Placement

Your kitchen altar can be almost anywhere in the room—on a countertop, on top of a cupboard or the fridge, on the table; you'll just want to be sure that it won't get bumped or broken in the midst of your cooking activities (but if she gets a little spattered with cooking juices, it shouldn't do any harm). Find a spot near the stove or oven, if possible. Many kitchen goddesses are pretty hot and fiery, and they love to be right where the action is (not only can they take the proverbial heat in the kitchen, but they thrive on it as well).

If you feel like doing a little minor renovation, you could hollow out a niche in a kitchen wall to house your altar. Or you can improvise a setting for your altar with a special box—ransack the attic or check out yard sales to find the perfect one. Your altar can be set inside or on top of it. Or you could take a trip to the nearest craft shop; it often sells lovely wild-looking twiggy birdhouses that make terrific kitchen altars.

The shape of your altar, as well as the decorations you choose for it, will depend in large measure not only on your taste, but also on the taste of your goddess (a primitive terra-cotta bird-headed goddess would probably feel more at home in one of the aforementioned wild twiggy nests than in a columned and frescoed temple). If you decide on an actual historical goddess, you may want to read up on her to find out what she'd like. Make sure your tastes are compatible.

Honoring Who You Are

One of the most important functions of your kitchen altar is to remind you of your intimate connection with Deeper Power. It also celebrates the unique gifts and talents you bring to the kitchen—and to the world—as a human representative of nurturing goddess-energy. What small objects could you include on the altar to express who you are? A painter friend did a small still-life oil painting of her favorite foods for her altar. An avid needlewoman cross-stitched a very female-looking background for hers (she says she was inspired by Judy Chicago's *The Dinner Party*). An attorney found a small metal balance, a symbol of justice, to dangle from the hand of her kitchen Athena, and a potter threw a tiny spiral-painted pot to rest at her clay goddess's feet. Writer friends have made books from paper, lace, or cornhusks to place on their altars; a teacher places a piece of chalk in her Hestia's hand; and a marathon-runner includes a tiny pair of track shoes from her daughter's cast-off doll wardrobe. Many of us include miniature broomsticks, silver pentacles, or even tiny pointed black hats to celebrate our reclamation of witchcraft.

If you have a special love for any particular animal, you can find or make a small one to share the altar space with your goddess. Collectors may want to find a spot for an item from their button or stamp or kitchen magnet collection.

Find ways to share your talents and enthusiasms via the altar.

Ancestor Feasts

Your kitchen altar connects you in a personal way to Great Mystery. You may also want to give some thought to your unique place in the unbroken chain of life by creating a special ancestor feast.

Most of us have fond food-based memories of grandparents or other close relatives. What did they like to cook? Were there any special foods they made just for you? My grandmother knew how much I loved her corn bread, which she baked in a special tin shaped like little ears of corn; she sent boxes of these cornsticks to me whenever she could. I can never get mine to taste the same, but it is a mark of my respect for her—a way of honoring who she was—to bake them in her memory.

Whom would you like to honor in this way? If not a specific relative, think about your ancestors. Where did they live? What foods did they eat? In a very real way, you can bring to life your blood link to these people by fixing foods that are connected with them and sharing the meal with your family. Your ancestors are part of who you are; you are the continuation of their line. If you have children, you can teach them how they fit into this unbroken line of life by involving them in these special ancestor feasts. Older children might want to research the foods and customs specific to the countries that birthed your relatives. Everyone can get involved in selecting and preparing the food. You may want to take a few moments before the meal to light a candle and say a few words about your special, unique heritage. It is part of what has made you who you are. Place a bit of your special food on your altar to honor your roots.

Decoration

Although the choices for altar decoration are virtually limitless, here are a few basics to get you started.

Candles. Candles become the visible reminders of the hearth-flame. Small tea lights in aluminum cups work very well, and they often burn for just the amount of time it takes to plan, prepare, cook, and eat a meal. Or you could use votives (many of them have food-related fragrances: apple-cinnamon, honeydew, pumpkin-pie spice, vanilla) or regular tapers or pillar candles. The simple act of lighting your altar candle before you start your meal preparation can make a profound difference in the way you feel about cooking. Just be sure not to leave it burning unattended, or you may end up getting a visit from the fire department.

Food. Our distant ancestors left bits of their meals at the feet of the hearth goddess. It can be soul satisfying for us to do this as well. Perishable items will need to be removed and replaced regularly. Those of us who tend to be a little lax about getting rid of the food before it gets nasty can stick to dried seeds, herbs, nuts, dried corn—anything that won't spoil.

Natural objects. When we include on the altar something from nature, especially something that is relatively unchanging like a special rock or crystal, we are reminded of how ancient the planet is and how brief has been the span of human life upon it. It's good to root our altars in the ancientness of Earth.

Seasonal reminders. The four sections coming up will give suggestions for seasonal goodies that you can rotate according to the time of year: seeds for late summer, a small squash for harvesttime, evergreen sprigs for midwinter, sprouts for early spring. What is in season now? Pay close attention when you explore farmer's markets, or take a walk outdoors and notice what the green things are doing, what's growing or ripe. The world is filled with incredible bounty and richness. The altar is a perfect place to celebrate this delightful truth.

Utensils. It can be fun to honor the utensils with which we cook. Dollhouses often yield beautiful miniature utensils that fit well on kitchen altars, or you can follow the lead of artist Tasha Tudor and make them yourself out of various materials: Her hand-made Victorian dollhouse features a fully equipped kitchen of her own creation. Small wooden cooking spoons are a favorite, but you may prefer a miniature eggbeater, a tiny mortar and pestle, or a wee food processor.

Incense and burner. Most of us don't burn incense before we begin preparing a meal because we don't want to mask all the wonderful cooking aromas. But lighting a special stick or cone of incense is a satisfying way to bring closure to the meal. (Many of us also find that it helps the dishwasher to get into the proper frame of mind.)

Reminders of loved ones. It can be a special act of love to include small photos or mementos for each family member or friend whom we'll be feeding. When we bring visible reminders of our tenderness into the kitchen, it helps us to cook with a joyous, open heart.

Consecration

An important part of creating your altar is taking a few moments to bless or consecrate it. How you do this is up to you. You could simply take a deep breath, close your eyes, open them again, look all around your kitchen, and exhale. You could add a few words: "This kitchen is now a sacred place," or, "May the food that is cooked in this sacred kitchen feed us deeply." You may choose to do something more elaborate, sprinkling the altar with salt and water, smudging it with incense or a smudge stick, reading a passage from a poem or other work that has meaning to you. The important thing is for you to find your own way to say, "Here it is, I made this," to your inner self, and to the Deeper Power.

Making a Kitchen Witch Apron

Now that your kitchen is bubbling with holy and magical energy, ready for some soul-nourishing cooking to happen, we can turn our attention to our own witchy adornment.

Apron is a word loaded with associations. How many of us remember the fifties and those sitcoms where every woman was a wife and every wife wore an apron (along with a saintly smile)? Perhaps it's time to reclaim our Right of the Apron. Nobody relishes the idea of getting cooking gunk all over her clothes. Aprons are practical. And there are certainly thousands upon thousands of styles and patterns to choose from out there, many of which don't even make us look like Donna Reed or the Beaver's mother.

But what if we could make or decorate an apron that we donned like a high priestess's robe, an apron that expressed something essential about ourselves and made a clear visual statement about our magical cooking power? It's not hard to create or decorate a special apron. And it's not an endless project; you take only the time you have. The process is a lot of fun, and when it's done, every time you put on your personal apron you'll be reminding yourself (and anybody who sees you) that you're a powerful kitchen witch embodying the goddess in your kitchen. You may find that apron-decorating quickly becomes a party—get some friends together, pool your resources, and encourage and empower each other!

Here's how to get started. First, choose a basic apron style. Some people favor from-the-waist-down aprons. Some like their aprons with a bib. Others may opt for a full-body model that goes over the head and ties at the waist. Which style suits you?

Most of us don't have the time to machine-sew (let alone hand-sew) much of anything. But if you do, more power to you—you can imbue your apron with lots of personal magic, energy, and power with every stitch. Buy a pattern and sew your own. Or you may feel like trying your hand at clothing design—your apron could be patterned after a Kate Greenaway smock, or a Victorian pinafore, or a medieval tabard. Sci-fi buffs could go for a futuristic look. Or you could honor our primitive forebears by making an artificial animal skin that ties on one shoulder. Look at costume history books or historical paintings. Feel free to be as silly or serious as you like.

You may need more than one apron to suit your different moods. One friend has a fairly plain one for everyday, and a *Little House on the Prairie* kind of thing with hand-smocking and flounces for those days when she feels the blood of her pioneer ancestors stirring in her veins, moving her to gather wild greens for cooking or to make corn pone or biscuits. She wears bare feet with this apron.

Apron Decoration

For the majority of us who don't have the time to make our own aprons, here is an alternative that produces wonderfully satisfying results. Buy yourself a plain, off-white canvas or muslin apron—you'll find them in natural clothing or earth-friendly products catalogs, or at your local hardware, fabric, or kitchenware store. Then, using dye or fabric paint (or hand-embroidery or appliqué), color and decorate it as your spirit desires.

Here are some ideas, from the conservative to the outrageous. Use them as a springboard for your own inspiration.

1. Find a symbol or shape that is meaningful to you and incorporate it: spirals, triangles, pentacles, circles, eyes, pomegranates, animals, fruits or vegetables, wheat sheaves, flowers, weeds—there are no limits to the possibilities. What matters is for the symbol to feel important to you. You could make a border of symbols around the bottom of your apron, or place a large one on the chest (or wherever). You can achieve professional-looking results in no time with rubber stamps—look in your local gift or craft shop for them (or try the magical ones from Kate Cartwright; see the Supplies section at the end of the book). Or use stencils—your local bookstore probably carries the handsome Dover stencil books with designs that range from ancient Egyptian to Art Nouveau.

2. Find a picture that feels special to you and paint a copy of it on your apron—or go to the mall and see if they can do a photo-transfer for you. Some copy shops can do this, too.

3. Do you have a personal affinity for any particular colors or fabrics? This is the place to use them. You can cut shapes out of fabric and fuse them to your apron with iron-on webbing sold in fabric stores. If you like to sew, consider making appliqué designs.

4. Hot-glue guns make it easy to apply trim—buttons, ribbon, braid, raffia—anything that feels fun and right to you. The final product won't be washable, but this work of magical art doesn't need to last forever. When it gets grubby, it's time to make a new one—you probably will have developed some new symbols and colors by then, anyway. And you can recycle any buttons or jewelry to use on your next creation!

5. You could glue or sew on earrings that have lost their mates, or pendants, or entire necklaces. One friend sewed a long Native American corn necklace around the neck of her apron. (You can make beautiful necklaces out of multicolored dried corn. For directions on making these and many other magical things, see *Celebrating the Great Mother: A Handbook of Earth-Honoring Ideas for Parents and Children*, which I coauthored with Maura D. Shaw.)

6. If you love words, you can embroider or paint a few on your apron. Once again, rubber stamps—with many styles available for the different letters of the alphabet—could make this process a quick one. Try using the name of a goddess or Celtic heroine, or of any powerful, wise woman in your life whom you especially respect and admire; see a book or two from the Suggested Reading section and pick a name that resonates with you. Of course, since it is your apron, your own name would feel empowering, or perhaps the name of the persona you become when cleaning (see Cleaning, page 11). And we don't need to limit ourselves to names. Any evocative word that has a special meaning for you will work—the watchwords at the beginning of each seasonal section may give you some ideas.

7. Add wacky personal touches. A nearby friend has a Surprise Pocket on her apron, which she keeps filled with small treats for her children (the fee for a surprise is some help with a kitchen chore). If you enjoy choosing a tarot card for the day, you could put a clear plastic window on the breast of your apron to display it. Rubber snakes, bats, and spiders are the decoration of choice for one Halloween-loving friend, while another added a pink curly tail to the rear of hers.

Can you picture a bright yellow-gold apron with a huge tomato painted on it and the word BOLD or WILD or JUICY blazoned across the chest? Or an apron with a pomegranate on the bib, its seeds made of tiny hand-sewn garnet seeds, and goddess names in a border around the hem? Maybe you would make a tie-dyed apron with gold spirals and love beads (many of us remember the sixties with fond nostalgia), or one with graphics from a favorite T-shirt sewn over the bib, or another with appliquéed stuffed vegetables and eggplant-colored rickrack zigzagging all over. You are the goddess of your hearth—what would you like to wear? You have the power to create it.

And you can also create what you need. As my friend Rowan says, "Before I made my special Hestia apron, I really hated housecleaning—I thought it was the most dismal chore. But now, before I start, I sing this song that I made up and I put on my apron. It's changed everything. The fact is, my house may not be all that much cleaner, but I sure feel better about it! And that's what matters." Sing this to the tune of "I'll Never Fall in Love Again":

> *What do you do when you just can't start?*
> *You could put on the Apron of Hestia—*
> *Gird your loins and then the resta ya!*
> *I'll never hate to clean again.*
> *I'll never hate to clean again.*

For the Very Bold

Food and sex are two basic pleasures that go very well together (see the infamous eating scene in the classic film *Tom Jones*, for example). There is no reason that your kitchen witch apron can't be sensual or even erotic.

Feel like cooking something romantic, perhaps aphrodisiac, for your partner? Try wearing your apron and nothing but your apron. This sort of thing would work very well at Beltane, the first of May celebration of sensuality and fertility.

You could put generous painted or appliquéed goddesslike breasts on your apron. (One friend drew different foods pouring from her apron-breasts like milk. What the heck!) Or for the truly adventurous, paint a vulva in the appropriate spot—you could be the Sheela-na-gig of the kitchen. (Sheelas are wonderful female figures who have been proudly displaying their vulvas for centuries, many of them in carvings on old Irish churches, of all places.) Find your own ways to be daring and risqué in the kitchen!

Kitchen Rituals

Now that your kitchen is glowing with magic, and you're robed like a priestess in the sacred apron of the kitchen witch, it's time to look at the *spirit* of cooking—and ways for us to access a joyful and positive sense of that spirit, for the good of all. Some traditions teach that you should cook only if your heart is open and filled with joy. As one friend tersely put it, "Well, if I waited for that, my family would starve." The truth is, we can't always be in a great mood when we cook. But it is also true that just as food is made not only of chemicals but also of life-energy, so the food you cook is imbued with your own energy—the mood you're in, your state of mind and spirit.

The greatest gift you can give yourself and anyone who eats your food is a few moments of time-out before you begin, time to relax, to breathe deeply and with attention, time to heal from the stresses of the day. Kitchen rituals are ways to help you do this. More than anything else, the creation and performance of simple kitchen rituals will help you to connect with the Goddess, with the magic of the Earth, so that you can cook like a true witch in your kitchen.

A ritual is any action performed with intention. Although the word has come to mean elaborate, repetitive, and probably arcane rites, it really means something much simpler. Rituals are meant to alter our awareness, to bring us into a deeper mode of being or perceiving. Ritual activity before we cook will help us to approach cooking in a more mindful, sacred way. But this never needs to be a solemn thing (unless you'd like it to be), and certainly not a pretentious one. Your kitchen ritual may be nothing more complicated than taking a deep breath and lighting a candle before you begin to cook—but it still counts. And it still works.

Here are some possibilities, starting with my own personal favorite: the glass-of-wine ritual (some of us have been doing this one for years; we just didn't know it counted). Sit in your Power Place. Pour yourself (and a friend or partner, if available) a glass of wine. (If you are avoiding alcohol, a glass of some pure, fresh fruit juice will work just as well.) First, really notice the color. Hold it to the light and look through it, see how your kitchen looks from the other side. Now take a whiff and enjoy the pleasant muskiness or earthiness. Now sip it slowly, thoughtfully. Savor the complex flavors and scents. Is that a hint of black currant or myrrh? Is there an aftertaste of apples or spice? Imagine the ripe, smooth grapes and the lush vineyards that produced this wine. Outside it may be cold and drizzly, but the slopes where those grapes grew were sunny and warm. The fertile richness of earth and the powerful energy of the sun are in this glass of wine. Give yourself fully to the experience of enjoying it. When it is gone, thank it.

There are many other rituals that you can try or invent. One friend takes her favorite wooden spoon and taps on the countertop before she begins to cook, like a conductor before a concert rapping on the podium for the orchestra's attention. Another uses her precooking hand washing as a part of her spiritual practice: As she soaps her hands, she does a check of her present condition—emotional, mental, and physical. "Today I'm feeling irritable and stressed. I didn't get enough sleep because the dog threw up on the bed at 3 A.M. I got caught in traffic, and I didn't have time to go to the farmer's market, so we have to eat whatever's in the fridge." Then, as she rinses, she says, "That's the way it is. But now my hands are clean. I turn my attention to the food I have."

Try taking a moment to look into the face of your kitchen goddess. Imitate her expression. What is her body doing? Mimic her position. Notice how it feels to hold your hands and arms, your legs and feet, the way she does; most goddesses have very powerful stances. Now light a candle at her feet and enjoy the glow, the way it lights her face. Breathe deeply and quietly for a few breaths.

The final step of any kitchen ritual involves food. Allow thoughts of the food you have on hand simply to be in your mind. What hungers are stirring in you? What sounds good? Do any particular foods appeal to you now?

The seasonal sections that follow will give you lots of inspiration. You may find that the images, flavors, and sensual delights of each will keep you company throughout your year, suggesting many delicious ways to enjoy the rich gifts of Earth.

The Kitchen Witch Feast

What better way to celebrate all of your inspiriting play around your kitchen than by throwing a kitchen witch feast? The possibilities for magical fun here are endless. Prepare for it by taking a special ritual bath with herbs, oils, or sea salt. Put on an outfit that makes you feel powerful and strong—with your special apron over that. Choose a menu that honors your kitchen goddess. What would she like to eat? What region or culture does she evoke? Athena or Artemis may enjoy Greek-style grape leaves stuffed with rice and nuts and feta cheese. Irish Brigid might be partial to oatcakes or potatoes and cabbage. Then again, your goddess may be heartily sick of the same old thing—you could expand her food horizons and offer her something wildly different from her usual fare.

Once you've decided on the menu, make up a song or a blessing to consecrate your sacred and sensual cooking space. Revel in your connection to the Goddess, in the fact that she *needs* you to embody aspects of her that only you can embody. Together, you have created a kitchen where both of you are honored and at home. Celebrate!

You may want to enjoy the event alone, or you could invite your friends to celebrate with you; there is great magic in women singing and dancing, drumming and laughing in the kitchen. You may want to create a special Earth-loving ritual to perform alone or together. You may even find yourselves taking turns hosting kitchen witch feasts so that *all* your kitchens can benefit from the powerful energy you raise.

But whether we are alone or with loved ones, when we finally sit down at the table, we can taste each bite with gratitude—gratitude for the ways we make magic, for the vitality of our bodies that know the sacred in every cell, for the abundance of this splendid planet, and for the seasons that offer such delicious nourishment for our bodies and our souls. We were all called to this table. We can pause to give thanks for all the cooking and eating that are such a beautiful part of life on this earth.

Kitchen of the Goddess

I came to your warm round hut where the cooking fire spat and crackled.
You showed me the tower of brown bowls tilted crazy against the skin of wall.
"This spoon," you said, and put it, smooth from years of use, into my hand.

You scooped up something from a broad green leaf on the floor,
sprinkled it into the bubbling black pot.
Hesitant, I lowered the spoon into the stew or soup, whatever it was,
and stirred.
My muscles began to remember.
I stirred for a long time
and then I raised a spoonful to my lips—
the steamy smell drenched my mouth with moisture,
moistness flowing from mouth to mouth below,
and everything between was wide awake.
I was a baby crying for the breast.
I was open, I was starving, I had been starving for so long.
She held me in her arms as I ate. She was the ground.
She was the food. She was the spoon. She was the fire.

autumn . . . *The air has an exhilarating tingle, nights grow longer, and the trees gradually reveal their inner flame. In this season of change, we can feed our Autumn hunger with the help of these magic words:*

autumn's watchwords *harvest, thanksgiving, glowing, savory, bountiful, richness, golden, comforting*

autumn's scents and tastes *burning leaves, fresh pumpkin, the mouthwatering tartness of crisp apples or cider, savory onion and squash stews bubbling on the stove, apple pies baking*

Setting the Stage for Autumn

*T*he *perfect autumn house is planted* in a stone-edged field near the woods. You can smell smoke from a bonfire as you walk up the cobbled drive, your basket filled with apples from the tangled orchard across the lane. Indoors, you can still hear the insistent song of the stream, always on its way to somewhere, that murmurs nearby. You look out through wide windows ablaze with trees. In the field, a flock of geese rests near a deep, still pond.

The autumn house glows with thankfulness and a sense of deep security. The harvest is in, the larder is filled to bursting with food, and reminders of the Earth Mother's bounty are everywhere: the autumn kitchen has bittersweet branches or swags of grapevine crowning the cabinets, earthen pitchers bursting with dried weeds in all their fragile and fascinating variety, butterscotch chrysanthemums and wild asters blooming in salt-glazed pots. Pumpkins squat, heavy-bellied, on fans of brilliant leaves. Great wooden bowls overflow with autumn squash, and baskets of acorns and nuts load the big wooden table; apples, grapes, and pears spill from cornucopias; native corn, in a magical bunch of three, casts its autumn blessing over the open hearth.

The hearth fire burns with a gentle golden warmth, and you sit beside it for a moment to warm your hands and to gaze into the embers. What magical pictures wait for you there? What soothing, nourishing meals will you create from the harvest that surrounds you? When sunset comes, its colors splendid as the leaves' bright flame, you light amber beeswax candles to invite the sacred fire inside.

The Autumn Kitchen

*A*utumn *plays glorious hostess* to two special holidays. The first is Mabon, the Autumn Equinox in September, which is the pagan Thanksgiving. Although most of us buy our food from supermarkets, we still have a deep ancestral connection to the ancient patterns of agriculture. In autumn, our attention turns to the bounty of the harvest. And so the autumn kitchen is a place of celebration, a glowing shrine at the heart of our home that announces the harvest season with dried corn hanging on the door and corn shocks in all their ragged beauty rustling nearby. Nothing gives us more satisfaction than the sight of a warm kitchen filled to bursting with autumn's gifts. Deep inside ourselves, where our most ancient memories still live, we feel that winter will find us safe and well prepared.

Suddenly, food is also the perfect decoration. Visits to our local farmer's market become intoxicating adventures, but we need strong arms to carry home all the bounty of the season! Once there, we're faced with the classic dilemma: Should we eat it or save it to admire? Most of us end up buying more than we can use simply for the sheer pleasure of looking at it all season long—fortunately, most autumn fruits and squashes keep well.

Many of us have fond childhood memories of trips to the country in the fall. Nothing tasted better than the crisp McIntosh or Golden Delicious you munched as you drove home, car packed with apples and pumpkins and fresh cider. Making an autumn pilgrimage to beauty—opening your heart to the glory of the trees—can be a powerful experience, and roadside stands offer riches that taste especially sweet because of the extra effort you made to find them.

Mother Earth takes great joy in decorating the world in fall. We can share some of her pleasure—and ally ourselves with her gracious abundance—when we choose autumn decorations and colors for our kitchens. In early autumn, we surround ourselves with dusky burgundies and gold-tinged greens in honor of the orchard and wine harvests. You may enjoy stenciling or painting plump harvest pears or apples here and there, or devising borders of grapes and vines. Some of us can't resist displaying big bowls of artificial grapes (the real ones just don't last long enough) in all their fruity rubies, plums, and purples; a good fake can be a joy forever. Grapes are perfect little globes of autumn color, beautiful in and of themselves. But they also gently remind us that the hardships and pressures and bruisings of life help us to give our finest gifts; a cushioned grape gives no wine.

By mid-autumn the trees amaze us with their brightness. We can echo their passionate splendor on our walls, doors, or cupboards with splashes of garnet or burnt orange, russet, or gold. And here is a simple exercise that will deepen your appreciation of each leaf's beauty and complexity. Choose a single perfect leaf from the many possibilities outdoors. Then, using a pencil, trace around its outline directly onto a painted cabinet or wall. Fill in your outline with the most vivid markers or paints you can find, doing your best to echo the leaf's vibrant coloring. You'll find that copying something from nature is a wonderful way to relax a stressed or harried mind. And the finished leaf (which may look surprisingly real) will be an autumn-long reminder of the trees.

There are many other ways to celebrate the trees in your kitchen. You could string some autumn-leaf lights above your sink, or hang a few preserved leaves over the table. (Try microwaving leaves between paper towels for a minute on each side to keep their color fresh.) The leaf-copying exercise above may inspire you to paint swirls of leaves on the walls. Some of us have even been known to scatter an armful of real ones on the floor to soften the harsh corners!

It can be very satisfying to make or find special kitchen decorations as the weather changes. Something as playful and inexpensive as a scarlet and orange maple-leaf potholder or a set of apple napkin rings can add an autumn note of brightness to the room and to our meals. Autumn is the time for special family feasts; serving platters, plates, and bowls in autumn leaf or harvest fruit and vegetable shapes will become your celebratory feast companions year after year. (October just wouldn't be the same in our house, for example, without our special pumpkin tea mugs.)

The squash harvest inspires us in the kitchen with shades of bittersweet, creamy pumpkin, and muted greens flushed with orange. Your Power Place may need an autumn cushion in these delicious colors, or you could paint a harvest still life on a cabinet, or frame a luscious autumn botanical print and display it on the wall.

In late autumn, the pumpkins and midnight black of Samhain, the second autumn holy day and the Celtic Halloween, wind a cloak of mystery around the room. By the end of October, the leaves outdoors are mostly brown and scattered. You could echo this new somberness of nature's color scheme with umber, chocolate, and sienna along with the traditional orange and black. Such colors remind us of the fertile power of the Earth; even when she sleeps, fallen leaves become food for the soil.

When Samhain arrives on October 31, your kitchen altar may become an ancestor shrine, with mementos of dead loved ones, along with a traditional jack-o'-lantern, to honor this special day.

In western European tradition, autumn belongs to water, the element of emotions, feelings, relationships. Water's nature is fluid, flowing—and autumn is certainly a time of flowing movement: Flocks of geese and migrating songbirds, woolly bear caterpillars, and monarch butterflies all seem caught in a bright stream flowing ceaselessly away. It can be soothing to include something blue in the autumn kitchen in honor of autumn's element of water—a bright pottery vase, some lapis-colored native corn, or a cobalt roundel to hang in the window. Whenever your eye catches this blue magic, use it as a reminder to check in with your feelings. What emotions are flowing through you now?

This season urges us to look inward, to take stock, and to celebrate the strengths that will stay with us through the long winter ahead—our loving relationships and our own inner wisdom. Many of us have rediscovered ancient divination tools—tarot cards, rune stones, pendulums, and the I Ching—as valuable keys for contacting the deep wisdom we all possess. By finding space near our Power Place for a pouch of carved runes stones, a deck of jewel-colored tarot cards, or a special journal and pen, we honor our ability to see deeply, to make our inner landscape clearer to our conscious minds. Many autumn recipes take a little simmering or baking time. You can use this time to choose a rune or a card or to write in your journal. You may find that poetry sings itself through you at this poignant and glorious time of year.

Autumn Spell for Deep Harvests

In the course of a year, we do and experience such an incredible variety of things. What were our greatest lessons or most significant events? How can we incorporate them fully? If there were thorny gifts of difficult experience, how can we swallow and digest them so they don't repeat on us? Try this spell to make of the year's events a satisfying meal, a deep harvest of wisdom.

You will need a container for fire—a fireplace, fire pit, barbecue, or iron cauldron will work beautifully. Find some time when you can go deep. Take a moment to focus on your breathing; every breath is a taking in and an autumnal letting go. Be with your breathing, without trying to change it, for the space of several breaths. Now turn your attention to the past year. What were the major events for you? What did you learn? Take a piece of paper—you may want to decorate it with appropriate runes and drawings—and on it write down three sentences that sum up the lessons of the year for you. Read the three sentences aloud three times. Now, carefully light the paper and place it in the fire. As the paper flames and then burns to ash, give thanks for the patterns of learning, of taking in and releasing, in your life. Gather the cooled ashes and add a tiny bit of them to your next meal. Return the remainder to the earth with gratitude, adding them to your compost pile to nourish the future.

Early-Autumn Recipes

Apple-Squash Soup

serves 6

Apples are the perfect autumn food. Their tart, crisp flesh evokes the exhilarating weather, and their brilliant colors remind us of the leaves that give us their gift of glory for a few weeks before they fall. Paired with autumn squash, apples lend their sweetness to a classic savory soup, a golden beginning to any autumn meal. Served with wholemeal bread and a salad, it can be a meal by itself.

2 tablespoons olive oil
1 to 2 garlic cloves, minced
1 medium onion, chopped
4 cups vegetable broth (or more)
2 cups filtered apple cider or apple juice
2 cups acorn or butternut squash, peeled, seeded, and diced
1 large potato, peeled and diced (Yukon Golds are nice)
1 firm, tart apple, peeled, cored, and diced
Freshly grated nutmeg and ginger
Sea salt
1/2 cup light cream (optional)
Toppings (optional):
Chopped walnuts
Minced fresh parsley
Dollop of sour or whipped cream
Grated nutmeg

In a large soup pot, heat the olive oil and add the minced garlic and chopped onion.

Sauté the onion and garlic until golden, then add the vegetable broth, apple cider or apple juice, diced squash, potato, and apple. Bring to a boil, then reduce heat and simmer, covered, until squash, potato, and apple are tender, about 30 minutes.

Add the nutmeg, ginger, and sea salt to taste.

Puree in batches in a blender, return to the pot, and gently reheat. You may add 1/2 cup of either light cream or more broth at this stage, thinning the soup to the desired consistency.

Serve warm, with any or all of the toppings on each serving, if desired.

Nutty Autumn Salads

This is the season of squirrels—we can't help but be inspired by their busy energy as they gather and store the nuts of fall. Honor your own ability to harvest what you need—and make your salads more nutritious and tasty—by adding any of the following shelled nuts to your greens:

almonds • cashews • pecans • pine nuts • walnuts • macadamias • peanuts

The nuts may be chopped, halved, slivered, or left whole. You may also want to toast them in a frying pan or in a slow oven for a few minutes before serving.

Crisp Corn Tarts with Autumn Greens and Hazelnuts
makes 6 individual tarts

These golden tart shells make a pretty autumn picture heaped with succulent greens and topped with crunchy hazelnuts. Hazelnuts, traditional around the time of the Autumn Equinox, have age-old associations with wisdom and poetic inspiration. Shell a few for this special meal, but be sure to save some unshelled to tuck into a drawer or to string and hang on a wall.

You can find individual $1/2$-cup tart tins in cookery catalogs, kitchen specialty shops, or even your local grocery store. There are also tins available that are charmingly shaped like autumn leaves.

The possibilities for these golden shells are abundant. Besides the filling suggested below, you could also heap them with Three Sisters Harvest Stew (see page 48), stir-fried carrots, steamed broccoli—or just about anything your heart desires. Or you could roll out the dough flat and cut shapes with miniature cookie cutters (leaf, apple, acorn, and pumpkin shapes are seasonal) and bake as a pretty topping for stews or potpies.

For the tart shells:
- 1 cup unbleached flour
- 3/4 cup plus 1/4 cup fine cornmeal
- 1/2 teaspoon sea salt
- 10 tablespoons (1 stick plus 2 table-spoons) chilled butter or margarine, cut into small pieces
- 2 tablespoons vegetable shortening
- 5 tablespoons ice water

For the filling:
- 1 to 2 tablespoons olive oil
- 1 to 2 garlic cloves, chopped
- 9 cups (more or less) greens, freshly washed, coarsely chopped (this is about bunch, as sold in most markets; use kale, Swiss chard, spinach, turnip greens, or broccoli rabe; greens will reduce in volume as they cook)
- Sea salt
- 1/2 cup chopped hazelnuts

To make the shells, in a large bowl combine the flour, 3/4 cup of the cornmeal, and the 1/2 teaspoon of sea salt (more, if you use unsalted butter). Add the pieces of butter or margarine and the vegetable shortening.

Using two knives or a pastry blender, work the butter and shortening into the flour mixture until it looks like coarse meal. Sprinkle with the ice water and mix until dough holds together. Gather the dough into a ball, wrap, and refrigerate for at least an hour.

About half an hour before serving, preheat the oven to 350°F.

Sprinkle your work surface with the remaining 1/4 cup of cornmeal and roll out the dough as thinly as you can. Cut into rounds to fit six individual tart tins and press the dough gently into the tins.

Bake 10 to 20 minutes or until crisp. Allow to cool slightly and remove from tins.

Meanwhile, to make the filling, heat the olive oil in a medium-sized saucepan over medium-high heat. Add the chopped garlic and stir until coated with oil.

Now add the greens and cook, stirring often, until crisp-tender and fragrant.

Salt to taste. (You could use tamari, but it will discolor the greens.)

Heap the shells with the cooked greens and sprinkle with the chopped hazelnuts.

Three Sisters Harvest Stew   *serves 4 to 6*

This is a dish rich with textures, colors—and history. Many of the early Native Ameri-can people who farmed this land lived by growing what they called the Three Sisters—corn, squash, and beans. Then the first white settlers came. The newcomers found this continent harsh and cruel; winter brought starvation, sickness, and death to many. In a spirit of humane and openhearted generosity, the Native Americans taught the settlers how to grow these three foods. They became three gifts of life.

Three Sisters Harvest Stew is a tribute to the Native Americans who helped the early settlers to survive. This season, with its images of Pilgrims and Indians and Thanksgiving feasts, invariably brings to mind thoughts of Native Americans. When we make this meal, we call our attention to those few who survived the coming of the white people to their land.

This season is a good time to find out more about Native American issues. While the stew simmers, settle yourself in your Power Place and read a book about our gov-ernment's treatment of indigenous peoples. You may be moved to sit at your kitchen table and write letters to your representatives in Washington. Make your voice heard. It's too late to change the outcome of Wounded Knee, but James Bay and Big Mountain are at risk right now. Imagine the power of thousands and thousands of us writing let-ters from our kitchen tables as our stews simmer behind us. We can change things with our kitchen power. And we can take time today to give thanks for Native teachings, then and now.

2 tablespoons olive oil
1 large onion, chopped
3 to 4 garlic cloves, chopped
1 large carrot, cut into 1-inch pieces
3/4 cup butternut squash, cubed (for a quicker-cooking variation, use 1 cup yellow or crookneck squash, cubed)
1 can beans, drained (garbanzos, with their harvest gold color, are my favorite, but you could try butter beans, small red beans, or pintos—whatever pleases you)

1 cup dried giant white corn, soaked overnight in cold water and then simmered in boiling water until tender, about 2 hours,* or for a quicker version, 1 cup fresh or frozen corn kernels

1 teaspoon crumbled dried sage

Sea salt

1 dried chipotle pepper (optional)

Water or vegetable broth, as needed

1/4 cup chopped fresh parsley

In a large stew pot, heat the olive oil. Add the chopped onion and stir to coat with the oil.

Sauté until golden, then add the garlic, carrot pieces, squash, beans, corn, sage, sea salt to taste, and the chipotle pepper, if you desire. Though the pepper is optional, the smoky taste is reminiscent of the first hearth fires of the season, perfect for autumn.

Simmer the stew, adding the water or vegetable broth as needed, until the squash is tender, then add the parsley and stir thoroughly.

Serve piping hot.

---

* This adds a very chewy and unusual note to the stew. If you want to be really autumnal and adventurous—and if you would like to make a special link with the people who lived on this continent before us—you could use 1 cup of dried Native American corn, treated the same way. Buy a bunch—usually sold as a door decoration—at the farmer's market, break the cobs in half, and use a twisting motion to release the kernels. There are so many lovely colors to choose from! But please be sure that no shellacs or chemicals were added to your corn.

Simple Baked Pears

Pears smell and taste like autumn. Their sweetness evokes orchards of trees heavy with harvest fruit, smoke from bonfires weaving a spiral pattern among the branches, a golden sunset overhead, and an exhilarating snap in the air. And the pear's shape is so superbly sensual. Many of us delight in celebrating the pear as we gradually grow to resemble one, but on one occasion after enjoying several very rich pear desserts—a buttery tart, a cake drenched in pear liqueur—I realized we don't exactly need to hurry the process along!

This recipe rates next to fresh fruit as one of the kitchen witch's simplest creations. Instead of spending a lot of time fussing over a fancy (and fattening) pear dessert, you can use that time to take a walk outdoors and enjoy the beautiful autumn foliage. The pears will be done by the time you get back.

1   **pear, smooth and very firm (Bosc—perfect; Red Bartlett—the color is wonderful; or any firm variety)**

Preheat the oven to 350°F.

While your oven is preheating, take a moment to appreciate your pear (some recipes require a little foreplay). Hold it in both hands and notice its nice, substantial heft. What does the skin of your pear feel like? (Boscs, for instance, have a very dry, smooth skin). Enjoy stroking your pear and remember how its flesh can be as crisp as the weather; imagine how it would feel in your mouth if you took a bite of it now.

Look at the beautiful gradations in its color and skin texture. Did you know that Red Bartletts are dotted with tiny, differently colored circles? Now bring your pear close to your nose and inhale its harvest aroma.

When you have fully experienced your pear, stand it up in a baking pan and place it in the preheated oven. Set the timer for about 45 minutes. Know that when you get back from your walk, your pear will have been transformed from a hard, crunchy fruit into a meltingly sweet and tender one. What a lovely gift from the Goddess. Enjoy it!

Mabon Magic

*S*ometime between *September 20 and 23*, a moment of perfect balance between light and dark occurs. Mabon, named for a Celtic god of light, celebrates the day and night in equilibrium. After this day the nights will grow gradually longer, but now, for this one precious moment in time, the day and night are of equal length. Unlike the cultural Thanksgiving holiday, Mabon coincides with the actual harvest season. Traditionally, Mabon is the time to take stock of our harvest, to be grateful for our achievements and for the abundance in our lives. Before our annual fall feast, my friends and family often honor the day by making toasts with sparkling cider, naming all the things we learned and accomplished throughout the past months—and then we glory in the deliciousness of food and of life itself.

But Mabon is certainly not all sweetness and light. It also marks the time when the world begins to turn its energies inward, when we are urged to go deeper, to embrace the nourishing dark and its mysterious teachings, to honor the things that will encourage and sustain us throughout the cold winter months.

 After the most difficult year of my life, which saw the dissolution of a relationship that had been central to me, Mabon encouraged me to think of the year in terms of bitter harvests—life lessons that teach through difficulty, that make us strong. At our community Mabon celebration, we offered those bitter harvests to Kali, honoring that goddess of destruction and creation with May Sarton's wonderful poem "Invocation to Kali," because, as Sarton says, without darkness nothing comes to light. Afterward, we lit candles for each other with blessings for the dark months ahead, and then placed those small, brave lights at the feet of the great Harvest Mother. A perfect yin-yang, Mabon shows us the bitter in the sweet, the sweet in the bitter, and the mysterious ways that darkness and light dance together.

Kitchen Rituals for Mabon

On this day of balance, it will help us to stay balanced in the kitchen if we take some time to weed out the things we never use. As we watch the spiral dance of the leaves, so beautiful as they let go, we can take a lesson from the trees and learn how to let go of things that we don't need anymore—all the dusty gadgets, the electric bun-warmers, plastic spoon rests, and rubberized tablecloths that were gifts from the well and meaning long ago. Have a trade with friends, or make a donation to a battered women's shelter or a charity thrift shop. Getting rid of outgrown stuff gives us a wonderful cathartic feeling; it becomes a way of standing firmly where we are now and saying, "This is who I am."

Today would be a perfect day to make a place on or near your kitchen altar to honor autumn's element. Choose a special bowl and keep it filled with water throughout the autumn weeks. Notice how quickly the water evaporates; you will need to add to it frequently. So many of us feel dried up by the frenzied demands of our lives. Refilling your water bowl becomes a way of affirming your commitment to your own inner spring, your own inner source. You may want to float a perfect leaf in it. Or scoop out the top of an apple, place a tea light inside, light it, and float the flaming apple in the bowl.

The Autumn Equinox brings to mind the ancient Greek story of Demeter and her daughter Persephone, who on this day of balance must go back to the underworld, land of the dead, for her annual six-month stay. Food plays a starring role in this old myth. According to the rules of the underworld, if you eat anything while you're there, you're stuck in the place forever. Hades, god of the underworld, is smitten with Persephone; he kidnaps her, takes her there, and asks her to be his queen as he tries to stack the deck in his favor by plying her continually with food.

Now Persephone faces a big dilemma. On the one hand, she misses her mother and the beauty of the upper world; on the other hand, she wants to grow up, to be something more than just her mother's daughter. What to do? Persephone solves the dilemma by eating six pomegranate seeds. For each seed, she has to spend a month in the underworld—where she can be a queen, equal to her mother in power. And for the other six months, she can be a loving daughter in the sunlit world above ground. We can share some of Persephone's experience when we do the Pomegranate Meditation, below.

The myth also paints a vivid picture of Demeter's terrible grief. When her daughter first disappears, Demeter mourns her loss with rage and despair—the throes of the very first autumn depression. Demeter is an Earth Mother and when an Earth Mother gets that upset, the Earth is in trouble: Before long, everything is dying. Everyone from commoners to immortals tries to get Demeter to snap out of it, but nobody succeeds—until she meets Baubo, the first comedienne.

Baubo manages to get a laugh out of Demeter by hiking up her skirt and showing her vulva. If you have ever considered making or buying a Sheela-na-gig for your kitchen, Mabon would be a good day to do it. (Remember, Sheelas are those shameless goddesses who proudly display their vulvas. They make wonderful kitchen guardians, icons of the sacred gateway of life and the strength of female sexuality, and they offer powerful healing for patriarchal attitudes toward the female body.) Sheelas remind us of the belly laugh by reminding us of Baubo. You may get some weird looks from visitors (one friend saw my Sheela on the windowsill and

 said, "Is that a . . . ? Is that what I think it . . . ? Never mind.")—but your Sheela is bound to evoke some humor and womanly power in your kitchen.

Long before the Pilgrims, Mabon was the western European Thanksgiving, a time to thank the Greater Power for harvests of many kinds. You could make up a special blessing to say before your meal today. Persephone became a visionary—and a queen—through the choices she made. What choices have you made? What are your gifts? What have you done? Our works, like the glorious colors of the leaves, can shine brightly for a while before winter comes to teach us how to rest. Write a list of all the things you have in your life for which you are truly grateful, all of your personal harvests. When you are finished, fold up your list and place it on your kitchen altar with thanks.

You could also take a minute or two for this simple Autumn Equinox ritual: Stand on your kitchen floor with your feet about shoulder-width apart and your weight balanced evenly. Hold an apple in one hand and a pomegranate in the other. Close your eyes and feel the weight in your hands. Is one side heavier than the other, or are they about the same? Among other things, the pomegranate is a symbol of the descent into the underworld in autumn and the season's mix of bitter and sweet; the apple, of the promise of life's return in spring. Imagine yourself, standing between the two, as the moment of balance between light and dark, day and night, life and death. How can we learn to welcome the time of dreaming and rest as well as the time of growth and renewal? How can we honor them both?

Spell for Balance

Try this simple spell to bring balance to your heart and home. First, peel an apple in a continuous piece, making the peeling as long as you can, then set aside the peeling. Now fill the palm of your hand with dried thyme, a balancing and purifying herb. Slowly breathe in its fresh, pungent scent. As you exhale, say your name and the names all the people and creatures who share your home with you. Next, close your eyes and repeat the following charm:

Heart, mind, hands, soul,
Balanced, open, loving, whole.
For the good of all, so mote it be.

Now take the piece of apple peel and sprinkle the moist side with the thyme, rolling up the peel as you go. Tie the resulting bundle with string and bake in a warm (250°F) oven for an hour or so. The fragrance of the baking apple and thyme will help bring well-being and balance to your home and to all who live there. Once dried, the bundle can be kept to hold in your hand whenever you need a little more balance—and, if you like, you can enjoy munching the peeled apple, too!

Pomegranate Meditation

Pomegranates are magical fruits, not only because of their link with Persephone and her yearly stay in the underworld, but also because of even older associations with the female womb, the sacred chalice of life. Grocery stores usually carry pomegranates at this time of year; you could buy two and bring them home. Place one on your kitchen altar to dry and refrigerate the other to keep until you have a little time. When you do, retrieve it from the fridge, sit comfortably at your table, and consider this pomegranate. Red and a little lumpy, its globular shape is certainly womblike. Its waxy, smooth skin, when dried, will become rough and leathery. It has a jagged crown at its top, filled with tiny golden strawlike fibers with round-tipped heads.

With a sharp knife, cut a vulva shape gently through the surface of your pomegranate's skin—a curved diamond shape with tips pointing up and down. Carefully peel off the skin inside this shape. The inner skin is yellowish white; it clings to the seeds like a caul around a newborn baby. When this inner skin is peeled away, the vivid seeds are exposed. Take time to appreciate the beauty of this female symbol that you have uncovered and that the pomegranate embodies. Really look at the seeds:

Notice their translucence, their garnet color (the word *garnet* comes from the word *granatum*, the Latin for pomegranate). If you cut one, it bleeds. It has a subtle scent. How could you describe it?

Now pry one seed gently from its socket and taste it. (In just this way did Persephone taste her first seed in Hades.) Its outer flesh is cool and sweet, but the inner seed is hard and bitter. It is certainly both sweet and bitter to be a woman in our culture today. It is sweet and bitter to be a daughter. In what other ways can you describe the lesson of the seeds for yourself? If you count out five more seeds and eat them, think of them as your tickets to the inner world, the deep, underground wisdom that the outer world of frantic busyness often makes us forget. You have become a Persephone in your choice to go deeper.

Continue to peel away the outer skin to free the seeds inside. You can eat as many as you like, saving some to make Persephone Salad (see page 60). How do you eat your pomegranate seeds? Do you crunch them up, inner seed and outer flesh together? Or do you savor the sweetness of the pulp and spit out the seed?

You could take a small piece of paper and use pomegranate juice to draw a symbol on it that is important to you—a spiral, a pentacle, a triangle, a circle. You may want to place this paper, along with a few seeds, on your kitchen altar as a reminder of the pomegranate's teachings for you.

Song of the Mabon Goddess

Slowly, slowly she walks at dusk

Through village streets,

Serene in her deep red gown.

On every door she leaves behind

Ears of corn,

Kernels light as apple blossom,

Dark as decay.

Dusk deepens: her gown grows black.

Her hair is crowned with spiderwebs

That shine like stars.

Sweet is the savor of harvest

As night gains ground on day.

Take this blessing, friend, lover, kin:

Join hands with those who will warm you

As cold and dark draw in.

Mid-Autumn Recipes

 ## Demeter's Soothing Oat-Bread Soup *serves 4 to 6*

Bread soups were the nourishing mainstay of many a peasant village. Simple, delicious, and filling, they are the Earth Mother's answer to chilly weather. This special recipe offers Wise Woman healing for autumn depressions, with oats to soothe the nerves and sea vegetables (reminders of autumn's element, water) to nourish you deeply.

While you cook, remember Demeter's story. You could put a small bowl of this soup outside for her when it's done.

2 tablespoons olive oil
1 medium onion, chopped
2 to 3 garlic cloves, chopped
1 quart vegetable broth
$^1/_3$ cup crumbled dried seaweed (kelp, kombu, wakame, or dulse)
2 to 3 cups stale oat-based bread, torn into pieces (use homemade or farmer's market bread, or any bread that has real body; if oat bread is unavailable, use wheat bread and add $^1/_2$ cup rolled oats to the broth)
1 cup chopped greens (kale, collards, Swiss chard, or spinach)
1 teaspoon crumbled dried rosemary
Sea salt or tamari

In a large soup kettle, heat the olive oil. Add the chopped onion and garlic and sauté until golden.

Add the broth and seaweed and bring to a boil. Honor the sea and the cycles of the tides as you add the seaweed to your soup.

When the broth is boiling, add the torn pieces of bread (and the oats, if you are using wheat bread).

Turn down the heat to low and simmer, stirring often, until the bread has broken down. (Just like Demeter, but when *she* got depressed, the whole world died. At this point, take a look at your Sheela-na-gig and have a good belly laugh to cheer up both of you.) The mixture will begin to resemble thick soup instead of broth with bits of bread in it. If it is too thick and sludgy, thin the mixture with a little extra broth.

Add the greens and rosemary (for remembrance—think of summer's passing as you sprinkle it in). Continue cooking until the greens are just wilted.

Add the sea salt or tamari to taste and serve hot.

Persephone Salad

Garnet pomegranate seeds dot this pretty salad, made in Persephone's honor. All of us—no matter how close we were to our own mothers—have had to choose our own lives, our own separateness. With thoughts of mothers and daughters in our hearts, making Persephone Salad becomes a meditation on self-empowerment, wise choices, and the loving bonds of relationship.

Curly red lettuce
Pomegranate seeds
1 **or more crisp apples**
Persephone's Autumn Dressing (recipe follows)

For each serving, take a few leaves of curly red lettuce. The tinge of red on the edges of the lettuce remind us of the leaves beginning to flush and brighten outside our windows. Arrange the leaves beautifully on a salad plate and sprinkle with a handful of pomegranate seeds. (Use the leftovers from the Pomegranate Meditation.) As you sprinkle, think of Persephone's decision to journey deeper, to seek her power in the underworld. Think about your own inner journey at this time of year.

Slice a crisp apple in $^1/_4$-inch slices, *crosswise*. Surprise! There is a little five-pointed star of seeds in the center of each slice. This pentacle inside the apple is a traditional symbol of health, life, and protection—the Earth Mother's promise of spring's return. Tuck two or three slices of apple underneath the lettuce, so the edges are peeking out. (And be sure to hang a slice or two to dry; they make beautiful ornaments for the kitchen and, later, your Yule tree.)

Drizzle with Persephone's Autumn Dressing and serve.

Persephone's Autumn Dressing

serves 4

⅓ cup fruity olive oil
2 tablespoons fruit wine, such as
apple or an apple mixture (if
unavailable, use
1 tablespoon apple cider mixed with
1 tablespoon apple-cider vinegar)
Sea salt and freshly ground black
pepper

Combine the olive oil and wine and whisk until smooth. Whisk in the sea salt and pepper to taste.

Autumn Chard

serves 6

Chard, also known as Swiss chard, is a lovely autumn green. Like kale, it can survive a few frosts quite nicely, and the succulent leaves with their streaks of vibrant red are another vivid reminder of the leaves changing color outdoors. This chard recipe adds a creamy sauce to basic steamed greens; for those of us who feel a little blue in autumn, this soothing, nourishing sauce can be a comfort. Its nuttiness is another reminder of the squirrels' harvest and our own gathering-in as winter approaches.

8 cups Swiss chard, washed and
coarsely chopped (if the stems are
tough, remove them and reserve
for use in stir-fries, broths,
soups, or stews)
Creamy Cashew Sauce (recipe
follows)

Place the chopped chard in a steamer over boiling water and steam, covered, until tender—a few minutes at most.

Serve with Creamy Cashew Sauce.

Creamy Cashew Sauce

This rich vegan version of the ubiquitous béchamel or cream sauce is also delicious on many, many other things. Try it on cauliflower, spinach, toast, baked or mashed potatoes, rice, and sautéed or other steamed vegetables. (Or imagine an autumn version of Hot Summer Peach Play for Lovers [see page 179] with warm Creamy Cashew Sauce. It would be incredibly messy but lots of fun.)

> 3 **tablespoons olive oil**
> 4 to 5 **tablespoons whole wheat flour**
> 1 to 2 **cups hot water**
> 2 **tablespoons cashew butter**
> 1 to 2 **tablespoons tamari**
> **Freshly ground black pepper**

In a heavy saucepan, heat the olive oil. Slowly add in the flour, stirring to make a paste, or roux. Cook for a few minutes over low heat to toast the flour and give a nuttier flavor to the sauce.

Gradually add the hot water, stirring with a whisk (amounts will vary—the end result should be a thick, creamy sauce).

Stir in the cashew butter, tamari, and pepper to taste. Mix thoroughly, pour over the chard, and serve immediately.

Stuffed Acorn Squash
serves 6

This beautiful dish lends itself to infinite variations, all of them delicious. Try substituting 2 cups of chopped kale for the cubed squash, and corn bread for the stale French bread. Or you could make this a very quick recipe by microwaving your acorn halves (10 minutes on high power, or until tender) and filling them with just about anything you have on hand: leftover Three Sisters Harvest Stew (page 48) or Lovable Lentils (page 75), or one of those great packaged wild rice or pilaf mixes with a few chopped nuts added, or some sautéed greens—if it sounds good to you and you have it on hand, it will probably work. And the acorn squash bowls, besides adding earthy flavor and creamy texture, will make any choice look delightfully autumnal and festive.

3 good-sized acorn squash
4 to 6 tablespoons butter or margarine
2 garlic cloves, minced
1 medium onion, chopped
1 medium carrot, diced
1 celery stalk, strings removed, and diced
1 cup cubed squash (pumpkin, acorn, butternut, hubbard, or kabocha)
$\frac{1}{2}$ cup mushrooms, diced
3 to 4 cups stale French or country bread, torn into bite-sized pieces
2 eggs, lightly beaten (optional)
$\frac{1}{2}$ cup chopped fresh parsley
$\frac{1}{4}$ cup chopped fresh sage (or 1 to 2 tablespoons crumbled dried leaf sage)
$\frac{1}{3}$ cup chopped nuts (optional)
2 cups (or more) vegetable broth, salted
1 cup (or more) hot apple cider or sweet white wine (optional)

Preheat the oven to 350°F.

Wash the whole acorn squash and cut them into halves lengthwise. (This will make six bowls.) Remove the seeds and stringy stuff and set aside the cleaned acorn halves.

In a heavy skillet, heat the butter or margarine. Add the garlic, onion, carrot, celery, cubed squash, and mushrooms. Sauté this mixture over medium-high heat until vegetables are tender.

In a large bowl, mix the bread pieces, eggs (these give great texture to the final product), parsley, sage, and chopped nuts, if desired.

Add the bread mixture to the sautéed vegetables and stir to mix thoroughly, then add the vegetable broth (salted to taste). Continue to mix, squishing with your hands if you like, and adding broth as necessary, until the stuffing is very moist and soft.

Mound the stuffing into the squash halves, place the stuffed squash bowls on a large baking sheet, cover with foil, and bake until the squash is tender and the stuffing is done, about 1 hour. Or you could place stuffed squash in a baking dish into which you have poured a cup or more of hot apple cider or sweet white wine, leave halves uncovered, and baste every 15 minutes with pan juices until done.

Serve hot.

Fig-Apple Crumble

The voluptuous shapes of ripe figs—along with their Mediterranean associations—remind us of the bounty of Earth Mother Demeter, making figs perfect partners to the autumn apples in this homey, comforting dish. As it cooks, enjoy the divine perfume—an aroma bound to evoke home, hearth, nurturing, and safety.

1 cup dried figs, stemmed and quartered

3 large, firm apples, cored and cut into slices or chunks

$1/4$ cup plus $1/3$ cup packed brown sugar

2 tablespoons butter or margarine, melted

1 tablespoon plus $1/2$ cup unbleached white flour

$1/4$ teaspoon plus $1/2$ teaspoon cinnamon

$1/2$ cup whole wheat flour

$1/4$ teaspoon sea salt, or to taste

$1/2$ cup butter or margarine, cut into small pieces

Place the figs in a small bowl with enough hot water to cover. Let steep until softened, about 20 minutes. Drain thoroughly.

Preheat the oven to 350°F. Butter a 2-inch-deep, 8-inch square baking pan.

In a large mixing bowl, mix the apples, $1/4$ cup of the packed brown sugar, 2 tablespoons of butter, 1 tablespoon of the unbleached white flour, and $1/4$ teaspoon of the cinnamon. Transfer apples to the buttered baking dish and arrange the figs evenly over them.

To make the topping, in another mixing bowl combine the whole wheat flour, the $1/2$ cup of unbleached white flour, the $1/3$ cup of brown sugar, $1/2$ teaspoon of the cinnamon, or to taste, and the sea salt to taste. Using a pastry blender or two knives, cut in the $1/2$ cup of butter until the mixture resembles coarse meal. Sprinkle the topping over the apples and figs.

Bake until the topping is golden and apples are tender, about 50 minutes. Serve warm.

Samhain Magic

*T*he ancient Celts called Halloween by a different name. To them it was Samhain: New Year's Eve, a celebration of the dead, and a day for magic and divination all in one. Christianized western Europeans called the day that followed it All-Hallows and observed it with masses and mourning for the departed. Modern-day Mexicans call it the Day of the Dead, a day for partying and tidying the graves of relatives, eating skulls made of sugar, and leaving offerings for departed loved ones.

Today, the abundance of witch figures may remind us of a time long ago when the Crone or Wise Woman was revered instead of feared; glimmering jack-o'-lanterns are dim echoes of the candlelit spirit-guides that welcomed back dead relations for a little visit. Halloween, like several of our cultural holidays, still has some of the magical husk surrounding it, although much of the real juice has been drained away. But with the help of the Kitchen Goddess (and a little autumn water-magic), we can refill Samhain from the sacred spring that never runs dry.

Samhain is both mysterious and friendly, an opportunity for us to come to an amicable understanding with death. In our culture—at once violent, death-haunted, and death-denying—we are taught to hate and fear death. Samhain helps us to make friends with death—and to honor Mystery.

Death can come in many forms. For years, my Samhain revolved around creating magical costumes with my young son for his trick-or-treat journey, and playing the divination games with him that would guide us in the coming year. This past Samhain, while my son, now a teenager, went out on the town with a can of shaving cream, my new sweetheart and I made an altar in the fireplace with photos of his father, who had died a month earlier. But I also went deep into my own dark: In the crumbling stone fireplace of the dirt-floored, rather creepy cellar in this old Colonial house, I made an altar. In it, I placed pictures of my son, his father, and me—reminders of my old family structure that has died. Giving myself time and space to grieve the loss of my old partnership was a healing way to begin the new year. By honoring death, we begin to build new lives over the bones of the old.

Kitchen Rituals for Samhain

We can start re-creating the Halloween holiday in the kitchen. Some of us like to hide little *memento mori* throughout the room on Samhain. Then, whenever we open a drawer—surprise!—there's a skull grinning up at us! Skeletons may lurk among the chrysanthemums, or peek out from behind the butternuts, or dangle from a cabinet-pull, or sit with legs casually crossed on the plates inside dark cupboards. The element of the unexpected adds a lot to these gentle, humorous reminders of mortality.

Our kitchen altars are the right place for old photos or keepsakes that remind us of those who have died; Samhain is the time for making ancestor shrines, in the kitchen or anywhere else. Who were your relations? Where did they come from? How did they cook and what foods did they eat?

Today is the perfect day to set the table with those old plates or glasses that were left to you by your grandmother, your aunt, or your mother. Or try using some of their

utensils. If you juice the lemon for Autumn Cider Dressing with an old wooden reamer—one that was held and used by hands that you loved—it will be a much more meaningful process than simply getting out the electric juicer.

You could design an entire meal around the favorite recipes of your dead loved ones (see Ancestor Feasts, page 25). Set an extra place for anyone who has died in the past year, or for a special relative or friend. Tell loving stories about them at dinner.

Spell to Bless the Bones

At Samhain, when our thoughts just naturally turn to skeletons, we perform this spell to send a message of healing, health, and wholeness to our bones, magically made of the earth's minerals, the firm structure that gives us fundamental support. You may want to do this together with your family. Encourage younger children to touch each of their bones as you name them. You may also perform this spell on your loved ones, placing your hands gently on each area and sending loving energy into each bone.

Stand with your knees flexed, about shoulder-width apart, and begin to sway gently from foot to foot, back and forth, quietly, rhythmically. Bring your awareness to the bones of your feet. There are many, many of them. They are your primary place of connection to the Earth. As you sway, say these words, aloud or to yourself:

Bless you, bones of my feet.

Now become aware of your ankle bones, shin bones, knees, thigh bones. These bones help you get from place to place:

Bless you, bones of my legs.

Bring attention to your spine, hips, ribs. These bones cradle your organs and keep you upright.

Bless you, bones of my trunk.

Now bring your consciousness to your collarbone, shoulders, upper arms, elbows,

lower arms, wrists, and hands. So many bones. These bones help you to do—to cook, to eat, to please others, to please yourself.

> *Bless you, bones of my arms and hands.*

Now hold your neck and skull in your magical awareness. These bones support and hold the wondrous head, seat of so many senses.

> *Bless you, bones of my neck and head.*
> *Strength and healing to my bones.*
> *May they serve my soul's purpose and support me on my path.*
> *Blessed be, blessed bones.*

Scrying Brew and Scrying Meditation

Samhain is the prime time for deep seeing, divination, magical workings and rituals of all kinds. Instead of making Halloween a holiday focused on sugar and scariness, we can remember the sacred roots of this night and try the following magical recipe.

Scrying Brew
serves 1

The ancient Celts knew that spirits were abroad on Samhain, that magic was as thick as sweet-smelling smoke, perfuming the air with possibilities. This Celtic New Year's Eve is the perfect night for divination. The loving ancestors who surround you like a warm cloak to keep away the winter chill will look into the future with you to see what gifts and lessons lie in store, what choices you can make to ease the way.

While many of us spend time with our runes and tarot cards tonight, there is an even simpler way to dialogue with the inner self, something that doesn't require any purchased cards, stones, or other props. It's called *scrying*, and it's something our own ancestors knew how to do. Scrying is simply gazing at any dark surface until mental chatter ceases and consciousness shifts. Wisdom may come in the form of actual images that seem to take shape on the surface, or pictures or words that form in your mind. Just about anything can be used as a scrying surface—the much-touted crystal ball is one possibility, as are elaborate scrying mirrors. But even simple country people knew how to scry using pools of water, bowls of broth—or cups of tea. The special tea below will actually help you to scry. Its primary ingredient, the herb mugwort, is the divination ally of choice; so you can drink most of what's in your cup and then scry in the remainder. Happy Samhain!

The herbs used in this tea are available from your local natural foods store, or from herbal companies by mail (see Supplies).

1 **cup water**
3 **tablespoons or more dried mugwort (not only good for helping us to contact our inner wisdom, but also very relaxing)**
1/4 **cup dried oatstraw (good for the nerves; if the Halloween partying and trick-or-treating have left you feeling frazzled, oatstraw will be a comfort)**
1 **cinnamon stick, 2 to 3 inches long (for its delicious flavor)**

Maple syrup, honey, or brown sugar (optional)

Boil the water, then add to a teapot into which the mugwort, oatstraw, and cinnamon stick have been placed.

Steep for at least 15 minutes. Strain and pour into a dark-colored mug, preferably black. Sweeten with maple syrup, honey, or brown sugar, if desired.

Now, sit comfortably in your Power Place with your mug. Sniff your Scrying Brew, feeling the steam, warm as breath, on your face. Take a sip and savor the earthy taste. As you sip, become aware of your breathing. Is it shallow or deep, quick or slow? As you drink, be with your breath without attempting to change it. When the tea is nearly gone, gradually turn your attention to the surface of the liquid remaining in your mug. Gaze at it without effort, simply letting yourself be with the mug and the tea. The disk where tea meets air may look silvery if it catches a light's

 reflection. As you look, pay some dreamy attention to the thoughts that flash through your mind like fish. What are they? All over the world, people are scrying and dreaming tonight. What images do you see? Take as much time as you can. You may want to leave the remainder of the tea in its mug on your kitchen altar as an offering for your long-forgotten kindred who knew how to perform this ancient ritual.

Song of the Samhain Goddess

Deep night in the forest,

Deep night on the hill.

The Old Wise One opens her cloak—

Inside, bitter smoke coils like a snake.

Heaped at her feet, orange pumpkins grin.

The bones of her hand shine through the skin.

Breath of Mystery rides the wind:

Honor me.

Breath of death cold on the back of your neck:

Honor me.

Breath of magic whirls around you:

Honor me.

Breath of endings and beginnings, always new.

Honor me now

Late-Autumn Recipes

Cailleach (Kale-Leek) Soup

serves 6 to 8

The Cailleach is a Celtic crone, or older Wise Woman figure. Samhain is her night; her strength grows with the setting sun. Picture her standing atop a seaside cliff, hooded, mysterious, her cloak swirling around her as the wind rises, frost on its breath. We can imagine the Cailleach (like her relative Cerridwen) stirring a huge cauldron, a cauldron of inspiration and rebirth.

On this crone's night of the year, as the old year dies, make this nourishing soup to strengthen you for your own journey into Mystery. As you stir your small cauldron, remember that you are the Cailleach's sister; infuse the soup with your own goddess's strength.

2 **tablespoons butter or olive oil**
3 **leeks, white parts only, washed well to remove grit, sliced into $1/2$-inch rounds.**
1 **garlic clove, chopped**
8 **cups vegetable broth**
2 **cups coarsely chopped kale**

In a large soup pot, heat the butter or olive oil. Add the leeks—the white, round disks magical reminders of the moon in your Samhain cauldron—and the chopped garlic. When the leeks and garlic are golden, add the vegetable broth and bring to a boil. Turn down the heat and simmer, covered, until the leeks are tender, about 15 minutes. Then add the chopped kale.

Stir your soup (with an old wooden spoon, if you have one), and as you stir, visualize your own croning process. There are many, many women on the verge of croning now. Embrace your wisdom, your strength, and your passionate convictions. The Cailleach will help to show you the way.

Allow the soup to simmer until the kale is tender.

Serve hot in a dark-colored bowl. Float a special autumn leaf on top, if you like. Although you can't eat the leaf, its color and shape will feed your soul.

Apple Salad

Apples have a long-standing relationship with Samhain. For centuries apples were used on this night to foretell the future—and to create a lot of excitement and fun. You could try some traditional apple play as you get ready to make this special salad. Twist the stem of your salad apple while rapidly reciting the alphabet. The letter you say when the stem breaks off is said to be the initial of your true love. If you're already happily mated, then make up something for your initial (let's see, I got an *h*, so I'm going to be wildly *happy* and *harmonious*. Or a *u* could mean I'm *uppity* or *unabashed*—you get the idea).

Autumn Cider Dressing (recipe follows)

1 tart, firm red apple, cored and cut into ½-inch chunks

3 cups (more or less) romaine lettuce, washed, trimmed, and torn into bite-sized pieces (you may substitute endive or red lettuce—whatever strikes your fancy)

1 cup arugula, washed and torn into bite-sized pieces (or use watercress instead)

3 tablespoons walnuts, coarsely chopped (you could substitute pecans)

In a small bowl, toss the apple chunks with 2 tablespoons of Autumn Cider Dressing. Place the lettuce and arugula in a large salad bowl and toss with the remaining dressing.

Divide the greens among six salad plates, top with the apples, and on the sprinkle walnuts.

Autumn Cider Dressing

$^1/_4$ cup fruity olive oil

1 tablespoon apple cider

1 tablespoons cider vinegar

2 teaspoons freshly squeezed lemon juice

1 teaspoon Dijon-style mustard

1 garlic clove, crushed

$^1/_8$ teaspoon crumbled dried thyme

Whisk all the ingredients in a bowl until creamy.

Sweet Potato–Apple Bake

serves 6

This is a quintessential autumn dish, a colorful and tasty reminder of the Earth Mother's richness at this time of year. Many of us grew up with canned, syrupy yams (often dotted with marshmallows) at Thanksgiving; here, baking the potatoes with apples gives a surprising sweetness without all that cloying sugar.

6 sweet potatoes or yams, scrubbed and sliced into $^1/_2$-inch rounds

3 firm, tart apples, peeled, cored, and sliced

2 tablespoons olive oil

$^1/_4$ teaspoon cinnamon

$^1/_8$ teaspoon ground cloves

Sea salt (optional)

Preheat the oven to 350°F.

Place the sweet potatoes and apples in a baking dish.

In a small bowl, combine the olive oil, cinnamon, and ground cloves and mix well.

Drizzle the oil-and-spices mixture over the potatoes and apples. Mix gently to coat potatoes and apples evenly with oil. Cover the dish and bake 1 to $1^1/_2$ hours, or until tender. You will probably find that this dish doesn't need any sea salt, but feel free to add some to taste.

Lovable Lentils in Pumpkin Bowls   *serves 6 to 8*

This hearty, warming pottage is made especially lovable with the addition of marjoram, an herb long associated with love. Marjoram also acts as an antidepressant, making this the perfect meal for these nights when Daylight Savings Time has done away with the evening light. Make a pot of it for the ones you love, to remind yourself of the people and relationships that truly matter in your life. (This recipe makes a delicious soup, too; just add more broth.)

4 tablespoons olive oil
2 medium onions, chopped
4 large carrots, sliced into ½-inch rounds
3 garlic cloves, minced
2 cups dried lentils
4 to 6 cups vegetable broth
2 teaspoons crumbled dried marjoram
Sea salt or tamari
6 to 8 small pumpkins, hollowed our and cleaned (optional)

In a large soup pot, heat the olive oil. Add the onions and sauté gently until soft. Then add the carrots—enjoy these round orange reminders of the Samhain season; their brightness makes a delicious contrast to the darkness of the lentils—and garlic and cook, stirring, for 2 minutes. Add the lentils and stir to coat with oil, then add the vegetable broth—start with 4 cups and add more, if necessary—and marjoram (as you add this herb, put your own loving feelings and thoughts into the pot along with it). Add the sea salt or tamari to taste.

Bring to a boil, cover, and simmer until lentils are tender, about 1 hour. Check toward the end of the hour and add more broth if the mixture is too dry, or uncover the pot if mixture is too soupy.

Serve in individual small pumpkins for an especially charming Samhain touch. If you don't have the time or energy to mess with scooping out pumpkins, you could always buy some pretty ceramic pumpkin bowls and reuse them year after year.

Moony Apple Pie

Samhain and moons just go together, perhaps because Samhain's traditions are all about seeing with the lunar self and experiencing moonlit and magical realms. And creamy, custardy things are the perfect foods for autumn, with their soothing texture and their associations with the element of water. This, then, is the autumnal version of a classic apple pie. The final product is moonlike and delicious.

1 **9-inch Classic No-Dairy Crust (recipe follows)**
2 **cups firm, tart apples, peeled, cored, and sliced**
1/3 **cup raisins (optional)**
4 **large eggs**
3/4 **cup maple syrup or honey**
1 **cup plain low-fat or nonfat yogurt**
1 **teaspoon pure vanilla extract**
1/2 **teaspoon cinnamon**
1/4 **teaspoon sea salt**

Preheat the oven to 375°F.

Make one Classic No-Dairy Crust pie shell. (With 4 eggs in this pie recipe, you don't need all the butter of a regular crust.) In an unbaked shell, spread the apples and raisins evenly.

In a blender, combine the eggs, maple syrup or honey, yogurt, vanilla extract, cinnamon, and sea salt, and blend until creamy.

Pour this custard over the apples and bake for about 1 hour, or until set. Allow to cool before serving.

Classic No-Dairy Crust

makes one 9-inch crust

My dear friend Nadine is a vegan (as well as a Wild Woman). She tells me her grammy, who isn't a vegan (but who may be a Wild Woman) has been whipping up these simple, delicious piecrusts since before Nadine was born and that they're the best vegan crusts ever. I agree. Double this recipe for a two-crust pie.

$\frac{1}{2}$ cup whole wheat flour
$\frac{1}{2}$ cup unbleached white flour
Dash of sea salt
Scant $\frac{1}{2}$ cup vegetable shortening
1 to 1$\frac{1}{2}$ tablespoons ice water

In a large mixing bowl, combine both flours and salt.

With two knives or a pastry blender, work in the vegetable shortening, then add the ice water, mixing quickly until the dough forms a ball. Wrap and refrigerate until ready to use. When ready to use, roll out the dough and place in a 9-inch pie plate. Voilà! Your crust is ready to fill and bake.

slowly, Mother Earth shows us her beautiful bones. In this season of cold, snow, and long dark nights, we can learn to rest and be nourished when we remember winter's words of power:

winter's watchwords Earthy, hearty, homey, substantial, grounding, satisfying

winter's scents and tastes Wood smoke, cinnamon and cloves, baked potatoes, evergreen branches, tangerines and oranges, spicy puddings slowly cooking

Setting the Stage for Winter

*T*ucked inside a stony cave or underneath the roots of an ancient tree, our perfect winter house is hugged by the earth, a cozy burrow lined with warm, smooth wood and roofed with snow. See yourself standing outside, knee-deep in snow on a moonless winter night. You're cold and hungry and tired. You have pushed yourself so hard that now you have no strength to continue. You need rest and mothering, warmth and deep nourishment.

When you lift your head, you see the warm golden lights from the windows of the winter house. You smell wood smoke on the freezing air, like the smell of safety and protection. Something delicious is cooking over a fire, you can smell the juices sizzling, the stew bubbling. Your mouth waters. Somehow you find the strength to get there, to open the massive wooden door and fall inside. Warm arms receive you. You have come home.

The perfect winter home of our imaginings leads us deeper into Mystery. From the heart of stillness, we create a place of nurturing and healing, a womb of warmth where we can dream while the earth dreams, rest while the earth rests. Inside the winter kitchen, it's always warm and golden, cozy and serene. There are blazing wood fires and soft cushions nearby, places to toast your toes and your spirit. Pots of richly satisfying teas are constantly steeping, and your favorite mug is close at hand.

Winter meals take time to simmer or bake, allowing you to dream by the window, luxuriating in the cozy warmth while the snow falls quietly outside. Deep quiet resides in the winter kitchen. You can hear a cat purring and the soft hissing crackle of the fire. Your tired spirit wraps itself in peace.

The Winter Kitchen

Winter holds a special holy day—Yule, the Winter Solstice—like a bright fire in the darkness at the center of the cave. Winter is the cave-time, and earth is winter's element. Earth is associated with the physical, the material—the body. When water turns to stone and the trees show their bones, winter teaches us about honoring our bodies, caring for them, allowing them to take a healing time-out from our culture's demand that we produce without ceasing.

We can make our winter kitchens into places of rest, security, and cozy warmth—and we can celebrate the austere beauty of this season in many creative ways. When we welcome Winter's colors and shapes into our kitchens, we are really honoring the sacredness of our bodies and of the planet. The pleasures of making visual connection between ourselves and our Earth Mother are many.

Before Yule comes at midwinter to deck our kitchens with evergreens, you may want to make a place on your table for a few branches of brown, dry leaves. Oak leaves, for instance, often cling to the branch well after they are withered, and beech leaves often stick around all winter long—so even the tardy among us can collect a few. These leaves become rustling reminders of earth-colored beauty, even after they have died.

When all the leaves are gone, bare branches can take their place in a vase. Arranging a bare branch or a perfect rock can evoke the purity and peacefulness of a Japanese Zen garden. Or you may enjoy creating magical little winter landscapes with rocks, moss, crystals (such wondrous bits of ice that never melt!), and twigs.

Early winter is a perfect time to make or find an earth-toned rag rug to stand on when you cook or do dishes. As you stand on its firm softness, think of your own ability to be rooted in the earth. And we can echo the browns, grays, snow white, and black of early winter in other ways, as well. Earthen bowls filled with smooth gray stones or deliciously scented, cinnamon-colored pomander balls, handwoven mats in winter colors, prints of winter landscapes—all help us to embrace this season of stillness and rest.

You may choose to echo winter's message of sleep by creating a soft burrow or nest on your kitchen altar, especially if yours is a hibernating power animal. If your favorite animals stay active during the winter months, you may want to put out some food for the ones living outside your doors (see Kitchen Rituals for Yule, page 95, for more on decorating a Solstice tree with food gifts for wildlife). When you think about it, so many of our images for winter involve beds and sleep: We say that snow *blankets* the earth; even sleet is said to create *sheets* of ice! We can warm up our kitchens and make them the perfect places to hibernate by including soft fabrics to curl up in. Our Power Place may need a special afghan crocheted by a loving granny, or a woven blanket in soft winter colors to pull over our shoulders like a prayer shawl as we sit and dream about winter meals.

When the Winter Solstice arrives, we bring our attention to the green that never dies. It is traditional and deeply satisfying to fill our kitchens with holly and the dusky evergreens of balsam, pine, and spruce. Evergreens are a feast for the senses—you may delight in heaping your kitchen with an abundance of sweet-smelling swags, garlands, and wreaths. And it can be merry to include a small branch or even a miniature tree on your kitchen altar. In the spirit of creating cozy burrows and nests for ourselves in winter, you may consider transforming your kitchen into a real bower of greenery, fastening branches overhead and all around. When you light a candle (carefully) in a kitchen brimming with greens, the shadows it casts remind us of enchanted forests and fairy-tale magic.

Consider hanging reminders of the sun among the green; oranges cut into quarter-inch rounds and dried make lovely sunny decorations, or you could string the dried slices along with bay leaves or cinnamon sticks for a sweet-smelling festive kitchen garland. Dried chili peppers, hung in bunches or strings, are another food-based Yuletide decoration, and cranberries are easy to string and hang, too. If you don't want food hanging around, you could make or buy small golden sun-shapes, which often come in beeswax and smell wonderful, to welcome the sun's return and to celebrate the promise of our own energetic reemergence in spring.

Greens in midwinter are usually enlivened by splashes of brilliant scarlet. Traditional holly berries, as well as rose hips, apples, dried pomegranates, and staghorn sumac (as well as the aforementioned chili peppers and cranberries), all add notes of bright color to our festive kitchen. Bright orange—in the form of clementines, tangerines, or the fruit that gave the color its name—is another color choice for midwinter, one that echoes and celebrates the sun. Many of us keep a big bowl heaped with these healthful, cheery little sun-mimics for any snackers to enjoy after a day of sledding or skating.

We traditionally celebrate the midwinter season with liberality and bounty, a sort of sympathetic magic to invite more of the same in the new year. We can incorporate gold and silver—those ancient symbols of wealth—into our kitchens with spray-painted nuts, acorns, papier-mâché fruits, and branches. Or we can go back to the roots of the custom and hide a few real coins in the bottom of a vase heaped with spruce, or tuck a folded dollar bill in a wreath made of herbs and bay and juniper, to encourage prosperity and abundance in the coming year. Take some time in the kitchen to think about the ways in which we are truly rich. Money is often the least of our many blessings.

But even more than the emphasis on undying evergreen and golden prosperity magic, the Winter Solstice season is a festival of light. At the darkest time of the year, we need reminders that the sun will return, that it will slowly strengthen, eventually bringing spring to brighten our lives once again. A few extra candles (especially handmade or hand-decorated ones) make wonderful additions to our kitchens. Tall seven-day votives in glass are often available in the Hispanic section of your local grocery store; just tie some raffia or ribbon around them and tuck in some springs of greenery or a few twigs.

Strings of electric lights, looped above the cabinets or wound around a wreath on the wall, can also be great fun. And besides the plain white or multicolored bare-bulb types, there are some great shaped lights to choose from: Chili pepper bulbs seem perfectly made for kitchens, and I've even seen tiny teapot lights that would look right at home over the table or sink. It is also possible to find lights shaped like various power animals (when he was small, my son's bedroom was brightened by a string of glowing fish).

But while it's fun to decorate with lights and greens, it is also vitally important to honor our need for rest and stillness amid the frenzy of the cultural winter holidays. As one friend says, "The whole place gets lit up like a casino at Christmas but what I really crave is darkness and quiet." Try to take a few minutes every day for quiet time. Wait for a short time after dark before turning on your holiday lights. Start a simple, soothing teatime ritual to welcome children home from school on bitter cold days, or create a late-night Dark Time for yourself in the kitchen—after you turn off all the lights before heading to bed, sit in your Power Place in the dark and breathe quietly for a few minutes. You will be surprised by the difference those few minutes will make.

In late winter we begin to think about emerging from our hibernation. You may want to include some opalescent colors in your late-winter kitchen to remind you of the ice that will soon be thawing, the snow that will melt into spring. One friend hangs crystal points around her kitchen in January like little magical icicles.

The kitchen is the perfect place for forcing a few flower bulbs placed in vases, bowls of water, or shallow bowls of smooth stones. If you start them in early January, they may bloom in time for Imbolc, inspiring symbols of life's dauntless power to return again and again.

Winter Spell for a Safe Home

This is one of the oldest, simplest, and most powerful spells I know, and I have used it to keep many, many apartments and homes safe and protected. Wait until after dark to do it, and give yourself time to go deep. A drumming tape may help you connect with the spirits of your cave-dwelling ancestors. For them, above all else the cave meant safety. This spell will help make your home feel like your own safe cave.

You will need:

a bowl
water
sea salt
dried bay leaves

Pour some tap water into a bowl. Dip your hand in it—experience water's softness, the way it takes on the shape of its container, its fluid and ever-changing nature. Taste it—does it have a taste? What does it taste like to you? Now pour some sea salt into the palm of your hand. Feel the roughness of its cube-shaped grains between your fingers. Taste a grain or two—it has a special astringent pungency. Salt is earth: mineral, solid, hard. Pour the salt into the water and marvel at the joining of elements, the way they mimic female and male, the way they permeate and change each other.

Now walk clockwise around the inside of your home, dipping your index finger into the saltwater and using it to trace a pentacle—the five-pointed star—on every window and door. You may want to chant something simple and powerful:

> *All within dwell safe,*
> *Safe from harm, safe and warm,*
> *All within dwell safe.*

After you have done this, take a few moments to visualize each pentacle shining with powerful golden light, setting the seal of protection on your home. Now place a dried bay leaf on top of each door and window, then sprinkle each leaf with sea salt. Know that these little talismans will be the good fairies of your home, keeping unwanted influences out and holding those within safe in a green web of protection.

> *Thank the earth and water.*
> *Blessed be.*

Early-Winter Recipes

There is an old wisdom to overeating in early winter: Just as hibernating creatures get pleasantly plump before they start their long winter sleep to ensure their survival, so our ancestors—worried about the possibility of food shortages and lean times—liked to put on as much weight as they could while food was still plentiful. While the harvest is still fresh in our minds and in our pantries, we can create special nourishing feasts, strengthening our bodies to face the cold weather ahead.

Early winter is pumpkin season. Not only are pumpkins rich in nutrients, but they also have become a symbol (along with the turkey) of the cultural Thanksgiving, which just wouldn't be the same without pumpkin pie, the quintessential American food. (Did you know that the early Celts carved jack-o'-lanterns from turnips, not pumpkins? Pumpkins were unknown to Europeans until colonists came to the New World.) But pumpkin has so many delicious uses besides the traditional pie. In this section you will find a luscious pumpkin-based soup, as well as a pumpkin pudding (which can also become a perfect pumpkin pie). Here are some other ideas to get you thinking about the beauty and flavor of pumpkins. But first you have to cook one. Here's how.

How to Cook a Pumpkin

A 6-pound pumpkin will give you about 8 cups of puree. This is a lot of pumpkin, but you can use it in some of the many ways suggested here, or you could freeze it or share it with your friends. Or use a smaller pumpkin—a 1^1/$_2$-pounder will yield only 2 cups of puree.

Canned pumpkin may certainly be substituted for this home-baked puree, if you're short on time—but this tastes so much better. And it is surprising how much more meaningful and nourishing our food is when we involve ourselves with it in this way. Baking a pumpkin becomes a reminder of the level of interaction that existed between our ancestors and their food—and if you grew your own pumpkin, so much the better!

1 6-pound pumpkin, or smaller

Preheat the oven to 375°F.

Cut your pumpkin in half and place the halves facedown on a baking sheet. (If your pumpkin is very large, quarter it.) Bake the pumpkin sections for about 45 minutes, or until fork-tender.

When cool enough to handle, peel off the pumpkin skin, remove the seeds (for a delicious treat, bake them for a few minutes at 325°F), and scrape away the stringy stuff. Then puree the pulp in batches and use or freeze.

Things to Do with Cooked Pumpkin

When we include pumpkin in our early-winter foods, we add creamy texture, earthy taste, and good nutrition (and your children won't even know it's in there). Try some of the variations on a pumpkin theme given below.

- Add $1/2$ cup or more of cooked or canned pumpkin to soups; stews; broths; pasta sauces; white sauce (it will turn a lovely color); or cooking water for rice, millet, quinoa, or spelt.

- Combine cooked pumpkin with the following and serve on bread, toast, or muffins, or use as an icing for cakes, cupcakes, or fruit breads: cream cheese (use more to stiffen it when making icing, less for a sandwich or muffin spread); maple syrup; honey; brown sugar; or applesauce; and pumpkin pie spices—cinnamon, allspice, cloves, nutmeg, ginger.

- Or try making open-faced sandwiches with cooked pumpkin and mashed cooked beans; grated cheese; chopped figs, raisins, dried cranberries, or cherries; chopped nuts; or toasted or raw pumpkin seeds or sunflower seeds.

Smoky Pumpkin Soup

serves 6

This unique and flavorful soup combines the perfection of pumpkin with the smokiness of winter hearth fires. This recipe grew out of a soup shared with friends during a cozy fireside lunch at a nearby Colonial inn. Outside, the November day was blustery and cold, but indoors the company was good and the pumpkin soup was warm and delicious. My friends tell me this version, with its unusual smoky taste, is even better than the original!

3 tablespoons butter, margarine, or olive oil

1 medium onion, chopped

2 to 3 garlic cloves, minced

1 small to medium carrot, sliced in $1/2$-inch rounds

$1/2$ cup well-scrubbed sweet potato, cut into chunks

6 cups vegetable broth

1 cup pumpkin puree (or 1 cup chopped raw pumpkin)

1 slice oat bread, torn into pieces (this adds body and oaty nourishment. If oat bread is unavailable, substitute whole wheat and add 1 tablespoon rolled oats)

1 teaspoon dried thyme

1 teaspoon crumbled dried sage

$1/2$ cup light cream or half-and-half (vegans may substitute soy milk or

2 tablespoons cashew or almond butter for a creamy texture)

$1/2$ cup smoked gouda cheese, grated (this is what gives the soup its delightful smoky flavor; vegans may use a few drops of natural smoke flavoring instead)

$1/4$ cup chopped fresh parsley

Suggested toppings (optional):

Dollop of sour cream, whipped cream, or crème fraîche

Small mound of grated smoked gouda

Grating of fresh nutmeg or a pinch of dried sage or thyme

Sprinkling of cayenne, for those who love heat

Spoonful of pumpkin seeds, raw or toasted

In a large soup pot, heat the butter on medium. When the butter is melted, add the onion, garlic, carrot, and sweet potato. Sauté the vegetables, stirring to coat with butter, for a few minutes, until the onion is translucent. Add the vegetable broth, pumpkin puree, oat bread, thyme, and sage. Stir to mix thoroughly, bring to a boil, then reduce heat, cover, and simmer until the sweet potato is tender, about 30 minutes.

Add the light cream, cheese, and parsley. Stir to mix and continue to simmer (do not boil) until the cheese is melted.

Puree in batches in your blender or food processor, adding more cream to thin, if needed.

Serve warm in individual bowls with a combination of any of the suggested toppings.

Winter Greens and Walnut Salad   *serves 4*

Winter greens have more body and bite than their more tender spring or summer relatives. Paired with toasted walnuts and mild red onion, this winter salad is a piquant contrast to the sweetness of roasted vegetables or pumpkin soup.

**Assorted greens, rinsed clean
(arugula, mustard greens, or
watercress; chicory or curly
endive; and romaine)**
8 **tablespoons chopped red onion**
1 **cup toasted walnuts**
   Olive oil
   Vinegar or red wine
   **Sea salt and freshly ground
   black pepper**

Toast walnuts in a 300°F oven for 10 minutes.

For each serving, take several leaves of each of the greens and tear into bite-sized pieces. Mound the greens on salad plates and sprinkle each serving with the chopped red onion and toasted walnuts.

Drizzle each salad with olive oil and a splash of vinegar or red wine. Add sea salt and pepper to taste, then serve.

Heartha's Roasted Winter Vegetables   *serves 4 to 6*

Heartha loves to keep us warm and nourished when the weather turns raw. This goddess of the hearth knows how to make a kitchen smell divine and how to turn the simplest ingredients into luscious winter fare. This dish evokes a red-cheeked, plump and homely goddess—a kindly, no-nonsense type—her sleeves rolled up as she cooks, her skirt the color of fallen leaves. Heartha wants to make things easy for us. Her Roasted Winter Vegetables are so simple to prepare—chop a few things, toss with oil, and then go take a warm bath or a nap while the roots and legumes cook. They end up sizzling deliciously, with crusty brown outsides and tender insides—simple, substantial, tasty.

6 **cups assorted vegetables, scrubbed and cut into 1-inch chunks—choose from: yellow onion, potato (Yukon Golds are pretty), sweet potato, winter squash (butternut, acorn, kabocha, hubbard), carrot, parsnip, turnip, or rutabaga**
3 **tablespoons olive oil**
1 **tablespoon dried rosemary**
2 **cloves garlic, pressed**
Sea salt
Freshly ground black pepper

Preheat the oven to 400°F.

Spread the vegetables on a large baking sheet.

In a small bowl, combine the olive oil, rosemary, and garlic (or omit the rosemary and garlic and use 2 teaspoons ground cinnamon instead) and mix well.

Drizzle the vegetables with the herbed oil, turning to coat vegetables evenly. Sprinkle with sea salt and black pepper to taste.

Bake for about 1 hour. At this point, remove any vegetables that are done and continue roasting the rest until tender, lightly browned, and sizzly, another 30 minutes at most. Serve hot.

Kale, Corn, and Onion Skillet Cakes *serves 4 to 6*

Corn kept many Native American people alive throughout the long winter months; dried corn that had been soaked and then cooked was a staple food. Today freezers make it possible for us to enjoy corn in all its tenderness, any time of the year. Paired with winter kale, it gives a wonderful, toothy richness to these hearty cakes.

A cross between a pancake and a fritter, these cakes are quite substantial and filling.

1 cup all-purpose flour
1 cup fine yellow cornmeal
1 teaspoon sea salt, or to taste
2 cups frozen corn, thawed
2 cups finely chopped, firmly packed fresh kale
2 large eggs
4 tablespoons butter (2 of them melted) or olive oil
2 cups low-fat or nonfat milk
1 cup diced onion

In a large bowl, mix the flour, cornmeal, salt, corn, and kale.

In a medium bowl, lightly beat the eggs, the 2 tablespoons of melted butter or olive oil, and milk to combine. Pour the wet ingredients into the dry and mix briefly.

In a large skillet, heat the remaining 2 tablespoons of butter or olive oil. Add the onion and sauté until golden.

Add the sautéed onion to the batter, mix again, then drop about 1/4 cup of the batter per cake into a hot skillet, adding more oil as needed to keep cakes from sticking. Cook until cakes begin to bubble, about 3 minutes, then flip and cook until the other side is golden, 1 or 2 minutes longer.

Serve warm.

Pumpkin Pudding (or Pie Filling)   *serves 6*

This is an undeniably rich dessert, but it is also undeniably delicious; after all, a few extra treats (and pounds) are always in order in winter. And Pumpkin Pudding translates beautifully into a perfect pumpkin pie—although you don't really *need* the extra calories of a crust, you could throw caution to the wintry winds and indulge yourself and those you love.

This is just about the simplest way ever to make a pumpkin pudding (or pie). The blender becomes a true genie, magically whipping up this comforting dessert with the push of a button or two. (To minimize the toxins found in dairy fat, use organic dairy products if at all possible.)

1³/₄ cups pumpkin puree
¹/₂ cup brown sugar
¹/₄ cup white sugar
¹/₈ cup maple syrup
¹/₂ cup sour cream
¹/₂ cup heavy cream or half-and-half
2 eggs
1 teaspoon cinnamon
¹/₂ teaspoon ground ginger
¹/₄ teaspoon sea salt
¹/₈ teaspoon ground cloves
Whipped cream (optional)

Preheat the oven to 425°F.

Just dump all the ingredients (except the whipped cream) into a blender and pulse until thoroughly combined.

Pour the mixture into buttered individual ramekins or ovenproof soup bowls—or the unbaked pie shell of your choice. (Decorate with little leaves cut from pastry, if you like.)

Bake for 15 minutes at 425°F, then reduce heat to 350°F and bake for 45 minutes, or until set. Enjoy the spicy smells that, like incense, turn your oven into a sacred shrine.

Allow to cool for 1 hour before serving. This is certainly rich enough—and scrumptious enough—all by itself, but feel free to top each portion with whipped cream, if you crave it.

Yule Magic

*S*ometime *between December 20 and 23*, the longest night of the year arrives to wrap the world in darkness. Yule, the Winter Solstice, celebrates the rebirth of the sun—after this darkest night, the days will slowly lengthen. The cultural winter holidays that share this Solstice time also focus on the return of light and life, the birth of something precious and holy. We discover the roots that connect all of earth's children when we embrace the Solstice holy day. It celebrates an event that is true for us all, no matter what other beliefs may divide us.

The favorite time for pagans everywhere to feast and make merry, Yule offers us opportunities to *connect* with each other. As we join hands to dance around the Yule tree, or share a goblet of steaming wassail, or drum to call back the light, or simply sit quietly together in the dark, Yule shows us the special magic of community. Even if you are solitary, Yule reminds us of the many helpful entities that surround us in the form of spirit teachers, animal guides, and ancestor wisdom.

You may choose to decorate your Yule tree with images of any of these that feel right to you. I like to cut out little pictures of my guiding goddesses, gods, and tarot guides, glue them on pieces of cardboard edged with gold paint, and hang them with ribbon from the branches of our tree. My son and I usually bake ginger-bread cookies in the shapes of magical cats, owls, mermaids, and wizards to deck the tree with as well.

One thing I have noticed in recent years is the longing many of us have at this time of year to *simplify*. Although Yule gifts are a delightful tradition, many of us are learning how to give without going broke or driving ourselves crazy. For example, one friend bought a selection of carved animal totem stones last year and invited each person in her community to reach into a pouch and pull one out as her Yule gift. Then she read each of them the spirit significance of the animal he or she had found, which—mysteriously—was somehow deeply right for everyone. Such magical simplicity lies at the very heart of Yule.

Kitchen Rituals for Yule

The Winter Solstice is all about honoring the dark and rejoicing in the light. Try this simple ritual on Yule Eve (the night before the Winter Solstice). Sit in your Power Place at twilight. Watch the world grow gradually darker. Allow the dark to simply be in your home, in your kitchen. Notice the small sounds that fill the quiet. Be quietly with the dark. Think of the fertile, nurturing darkness of the womb. What are you gestating now? What dreams do you have for the future? What do you hope to bring forth? Think of the Earth Mother, in labor during this dark season to birth the Sunchild.

Now, light a single candle—perhaps the one on your kitchen altar. What a great difference a single candle's light can make! Enjoy the warm glow. Really notice the different colors that lie at the heart of the flame. Make a wish for peace. Hum an old carol. The following song is an Earth-based version of a classic that we sang during a recent Winter Solstice celebration.

Silent night, holy night,
All is calm, all is bright
Round yon luminous Mother and Child,
Holy Infant so tender and wild.
Greet the Solstice in peace,
Greet the Solstice in peace.

Continue lighting any other candles you have placed around your kitchen. Then turn on every light in the room. Make noise, if you like. The light does return, year after year. We can honor the darkness, and we can be grateful for the light.

Now, as you walk the circle of your kitchen, extinguishing all but the most necessary lamps or candles, ask yourself, What are the lights in my darkness? What are the things that shine brightly for me? We are all alive on this planet at this moment. What a strange and wonderful combination of personalities and talents and gifts we represent. How can we shine for the world?

On the day of the Solstice, we can make a conscious connection with our planet by taking a walk outside to discover a kitchen stone—any rock that is pleasing to you will do. Bring your stone inside, wash it off, and place it on or near your altar to remind you to stay in touch with the Earth, to stay grounded and aware of your body. You may replace this rock every year on the Solstice, returning last year's kitchen stone to the earth.

Another kindly tradition is decorating an outdoor tree with food gifts from your winter kitchen. Such Solstice trees are a delight to watch, as squirrels and birds come to share the festival that humans have celebrated for centuries. Pinecones spread with peanut butter and rolled in seeds and cranberries; orange halves filled with nuts; dried fruit; ears of dried corn—all make pretty, delicious decorations for the animal people around you.

Today is a good day to perform a simple blessing over your food. Your body's own wondrous energy will do the blessing for you if you simply hold your hands over what you are about to eat. Hands helped to plant and nurture this food. Hands helped to harvest and package it. Hands cooked it. And the goodness of the food will strengthen us, hands and all.

Spell for a Grateful Heart

We live in one of the most materially abundant places on earth. Yet our very hearts are starving, always, for more. It is what our culture has taught us, so we will continue to buy, long for, buy, long for, in a cycle that feeds the economy but not our souls and leaves us with the taste of ashes in our hungry mouths. And yet what bounty surrounds us! We have more than enough to eat. We have homes. We have the means to learn and deepen and grow as human beings. We have a magical, mysterious connection to the powers of the Earth, to the spirit realm, to our inner wisdom. This spell helps us to be deeply *satisfied*—something we so rarely are—and grateful for what we have.

You will need:

A small jar of honey

Find a time and place where you can be quiet and alone. Bring the jar of honey with you to a comfortable spot (your Power Place could work) and sit quietly for a few moments, thinking about one thing in your life that gives you real pleasure. This could be something big—a lover, friendship, companion animal, creative work, magical activity; or it might be something little—the beautiful color you painted your kitchen cabinet, the taste of the soup you had for lunch, the socks with snowflakes on them that you're wearing today, the smell of the evergreens in the pitcher on the table beside you. Say, "I am grateful for this."

Now uncap the jar and inhale the rich, sweet fragrance. What an abundance of flowers and bees made this amazing substance! Dip one finger in the honey and place it on your heart-center, in the middle of your chest between your breasts, still

thinking of the thing that inspired your gratitude. Imagine your heart glowing with golden light, the sweet light of sun and pollen and nectar and bees. Say, "The sweetness in my heart shines for the world."

Know that this golden sweet light will attract more gratitude throughout the day. Every time you become aware of the honey's warm stickiness over your heart, give thanks for the pleasure in your life. You may do this spell for several days, focusing each time on a different source of real satisfaction. You may want to make a bee out of paper (or beeswax!) to put on your Yule tree as a reminder of the sweetness of a grateful heart.

Eating-the-Earth Meditation

This meditation brings us gently into awareness of the Earth and our bodies. It can be especially powerful to do this in near darkness, perhaps by the light of a single candle. Choose a time when you have an hour or so to spare; potatoes have a lot to teach us about slowing down and grounding ourselves.

First, choose a medium-sized baking potato, and preheat your oven to 425°F. Take your potato with you to your Power Place and get comfortable. Now, touch your potato. Is it gritty? There may be bits of earth, like tiny crystals, still clinging to it. When you bring your potato to your nose, can you smell its subtle, earthy scent? Imagine how the potato grows, underground in the dark, quietly swelling. Feel all the intriguing lumps and bumps on your potato, the little crevices and hills on its skin. Potatoes are as variable in shape as the land. Feel the comforting, substantial weight of the potato in your hand. One of these tubers can nourish and fill you for hours. Once, potatoes kept starvation at bay for millions of people. And when blight hit the crop, the people died.

Breathe with attention for a moment, simply noticing the pattern of your breathing, the taking in, the letting go, over and over, effortlessly. Now, as you continue to breathe gently and naturally, bring your awareness to the center of your chest. Allow that center to feel warm and open. Begin to think of the people alive today, this moment, who are hungry—some are far away in places you can only imagine; others

 live nearby. Think of the great blessing it is to have enough to eat. As you hold your potato, think of solid, practical ways that you can help. Do you have any extra canned goods? You could take them to a homeless shelter. Or you could volunteer some time cooking a holiday meal for the needy in your area. (Friends report that their most meaningful and joyful holidays were spent giving themselves in service in this way.) When we have enough, we can share what we have, whether it's a gift of time or food or money. Take a moment to breathe your gratitude for having enough, your gratitude for this simple, earthy potato that, in its unassuming but powerful way, sums up the food that is there for you whenever you are hungry, whenever you need it.

Now, really look at your potato. It has individuality, character. Its body will become a part of yours. This is the way of life on earth, bodies continually giving themselves to other bodies, eaten and eater in a circle dance.

When your oven has preheated, wash your potato, enjoying the way water brings out the smoothness of its skin. Pat it dry. Place it in your oven, and set the timer for 45 minutes.

In that 45 minutes, sit quietly in the dark and take note of how your body feels. Do you hold any tension or pain anywhere? Bring your attention to those places and simply be with the feelings there. Place your hands on each place, if you can, and breathe quietly, not willing anything to happen, just allowing the energy that flows through all creation to flow through you. If your body is feeling relaxed and comfortable, simply take note of that, and enjoy the pleasure of being without pain, without stress. Allow yourself to feel cradled by the warmth and the darkness. Close your eyes and dream, if you like.

As time flows through you, notice how the potato is beginning to fill the room with fragrance. The flesh of a raw potato is hard and crisp and pearly as an apple. Now your potato is baking into softness, into mellow creaminess. When the timer rings, put on an oven mitt, remove your potato, and cradle it for a while.

Is your potato steaming? How does it smell now? When it has cooled just enough to keep from burning you, place your potato on your body anywhere that you felt tension or discomfort. Enjoy the heat and steam soothing and warming your skin and muscles. Imagine the potato's sweet, earthy goodness penetrating all the way to your bones.

When you are ready, open your potato. What a burst of steam and whiteness erupt from the earthy darkness of its outside! Now sprinkle your potato with sea salt, and eat it. Savor each bite, knowing, as you chew each mouthful, that you are eating all the little hills and valleys that you felt on its surface before. The potato is a gift from the Earth Mother; know that its goodness was formed in the earth, of the earth. Know that your body shares the potato's earthiness—we are all made of earth's elements. And know that the Winter Solstice erupts with a burst of light and warmth out of the darkest time of the year, to bless our bodies and our souls with hope, renewal, and nourishment.

Special Festival Recipes

Even in this time of stillness and rest, the Mother of the Wild offers us nourishment for body and soul. Try the following special winter tea for a lively and delicious taste of the untamable green, and enjoy wassail with your holiday visitors as you celebrate the birth of new light.

White Pine Tea
serves 1

During the winter holiday season most of us invite the living green of pine, spruce, and fir indoors—in the form of wreaths and decorated trees, garlands and centerpieces—where their uplifting scents and vivid colors are infinitely cheering during these short, cold days. But we can also drink the energy of the deathless evergreen, sending its message of hope and renewal to our bodies in a very basic and earthy way.

The tangy sharpness of this tea is delightful to children and adults alike. The whole family can get involved in its gathering and preparation. Make a real celebration out of it!

If you're not sure what a white pine looks like, consult a field guide to trees. (This variety of pine has long, smooth needles.) Then bundle up, and go to the nearest white pine you can find (city folk may need to look in parks for theirs). Try to find one that is well away from the road to avoid heavy-metal contamination from car exhaust.

First spend a moment appreciating the beauty of the tree's glossy needles and fresh, pungent scent. Evergreens stand out like beacons of life from their seemingly dead and bare companions. Thank the tree for its gift of needles, leaving, maybe, a Solstice gift of a crystal or a special stone at its base, if you like.

1 handful fresh needles per serving
1 cup water per serving

Pick your needles (handfuls, like sizes of hands, vary; that's fine—everybody can pick his or her own), then take them indoors and boil the water.

Put the needles in a teapot and cover with boiling water. Steep, covered, for at least 15 minutes, then strain and serve with sweetener, if desired.

As you sip, think of this beautiful quote from Buddhist monk Thich Nhat Hanh: "Drink your tea slowly, as if this activity is the axis on which the whole earth revolves. Live this moment. Only this actual moment is life."

Know that this tangy, delightful tea is filled with vibrant green energy. This energy (as well as some helpful nutrients—especially vitamin C) is the tree's gift to you. May we all feel as healthy and strong as the white pine!

Wassail

yield will vary

This recipe serves a large gathering of moderate drinkers, or a small one of serious revelers, but measurements are approximate; the best rule is to taste and add, taste and add, until it tastes delicious.

Old-time western Europeans were fond of greeting the Yuletide with strong drink.

When revelers or carolers or merrymakers descended upon you, it was expected that you would offer a steaming cup of something to take away the chill. *Wassail* comes from the Anglo-Saxon *wes hal*, or "be whole," a wish for your visitors' good health and wholeness. What a much needed and wonderful blessing for our times! We can wish each other the same in a mug of wassail today.

This recipe is rooted in ancient and traditional Yule drinks, but it changes every time I make it. Feel free to improvise, so that your wassail will be as individual and unique as you are. Any way you pour it, wassail is a proven ally in helping friends and family to make merry, and it works better than any potpourri for filling the house with delicious aroma. You could make a smaller vat of nonalcoholic wassail for children and set it to simmer on the stove alongside the grown-up version. Just be sure—once you've had a mugful or two—that you don't get the batches mixed up!

1 **gallon (or more) apple cider**
1 **large cinnamon stick, broken into pieces**
13 **allspice berries (one for each full moon of the year)**
1 **apple, sliced crosswise (to reveal the pentacles within each slice)**
1 **small whole orange, organic if possible, studded with 8 whole cloves (one for each festival of the year)**
Irish whiskey (my favorite, but you may use other whiskeys or even burgundy or claret, if you wish)
Maple syrup or brown sugar

In a large soup pot, gently heat the cider with the cinnamon stick, allspice berries, apple, and clove-studded orange.

Then add the whiskey and maple syrup, to taste. Start by adding a cup or so of alcohol and taste to determine the potency you're after, adding more and tasting until you get it right or you're beyond worrying about it.

Do not allow the wassail to boil unless you want to lose some of the alcohol.

Serve steaming hot in mugs. You could follow an ancient custom and have your friends bring their own special wassail cups from their homes (just about anything will work as a wassail cup). As you fill their cups, add a few wishes for the coming year. Make splendid and outrageous toasts. Enjoy!

Song of the Yule Goddess

Ablaze in her golden gown,

A radiant Sun for her crown,

She dances the darkness away.

Awake and alive, the green never dies

And the dark always lightens at last.

So be whole, be whole, for the world needs your flame—

Burn bright as the night turns to day.

Midwinter Recipes

 ## Root Soup

This tasty, earthy soup honors the darkest night of the year with its own rich color that rivals the holly berry for scarlet brightness. Based on traditional borscht recipes dear to the hearts of those who live in wintry lands, Root Soup will warm your heart and your soul. Beets remind us of the Earth Mother's blood; their deep purplish red flesh and magenta juices are so rich in vitamins and minerals that eating beets becomes a nourishing infusion, one that is sorely needed around the winter holidays.

2 tablespoons olive oil or butter
1 medium onion, diced
2 cloves garlic, minced
6 cups vegetable broth
3 cups diced fresh beets
1 medium potato, diced
$^1/_2$ cup diced carrot
$^1/_2$ cup peeled, diced parsnips
$^1/_2$ teaspoon dried thyme
$^1/_2$ teaspoon freshly grated nutmeg
$^1/_2$ teaspoon sea salt or to taste
Freshly ground black pepper

In a large soup pot, heat olive oil or butter. Add the onion and garlic and sauté until softened, 5 to 7 minutes. Then add the vegetable broth, beets, potato, carrot, parsnips, thyme, nutmeg, and sea salt and pepper to taste.

Bring to a boil, then reduce heat and simmer for 45 minutes to 1 hour, until the beets and parsnips are tender. Serve hot. (Some may prefer to puree their Root Soup, but I find that leaving the roots in chunks feels more earthy.)

Pomander Salad

serves 4

Once upon a time, oranges were worth nearly their weight in gold and were especially prized around Yuletide. (Before the Crusades, most English and other western European people had never even seen, let alone eaten, an orange.) Rediscover the preciousness of the orange, shining like a little sun, that gives us its cheery fragrance and healthful vitamin C, Solstice gifts from the Mother-of-All.

This salad not only celebrates the orange but also reminds us of pomanders—oranges studded with cloves and rolled in spices, once prized as a kind of health protectant, deodorant, and perfume, all in one beautiful package. The delicious aroma of pomanders has always made my mouth water. Now you can have your pomander and eat it too.

Assorted greens (escarole, red
    lettuce, chicory, and romaine)
2 seedless oranges, sliced in
    rounds, white pith removed
1/2 red onion, minced
Pomander dressing (recipe follows)

On each salad plate, place several leaves of greens or as desired. Divide the orange slices evenly among the salad plates, arranging them on the lettuce leaves decoratively by overlapping them. In the center of each serving, place 1 tablespoon of the minced red onion.

Drizzle each serving with Pomander Dressing. Serve immediately

Pomander Dressing

1/4 cup plus 2 tablespoons olive oil
1 tablespoon red wine vinegar
1 tablespoon freshly squeezed
    orange juice
1/4 teaspoon ground cloves
1/4 teaspoon sea salt
1/4 teaspoon Dijon-style mustard

Whisk all ingredients in a bowl (or shake in a lidded jar) until creamy.

Festive Green Beans with Cranberries   *serves 6*

Echo the colors of the season with this simple, pretty dish. If you don't have any dried cranberries on hand, you could substitute julienned red bell peppers.

3 cups green beans, washed and
    ends trimmed
$^1/_2$ cup dried cranberries
    Melted butter or olive oil, as desired
    Sea salt

Place the beans and cranberries in a steamer basket over boiling water and lightly steam until the beans are bright green and crisp-tender and the berries are plumped. Serve on a platter, drizzled with melted butter or olive oil and sprinkled with sea salt to taste.

Savory Yuletide Pie   *serves 4 to 6*

Feel the power of the universe that makes the days grow longer once again, that brings light and warmth to the frozen earth. That same power flows through you. You can become the goddess Yula in the kitchen today, crowned with ivy and wielding a wooden spoon instead of a holly-tipped scepter. Use your hunger and your creativity to make a unique and sumptuous festival meal, a meal that will feed both body and soul.

The roundness of this savory pie echoes the shape of the sun, which we honor at the Solstice season with lights and celebrations of many kinds. The ingredients will be up to you; every time you make this recipe, depending on what you have on hand and what appeals to you, it will taste different, but delicious. (And you don't have to spend the entire day chopping vegetables for this dish, either. It is entirely possible to make Yuletide Pie with canned and frozen ingredients and a store-bought crust, if you're just too exhausted to stand over a chopping board.)

2 to 3 tablespoons olive oil

2 to 3 cups (when cooked) diced vegetables—choose from: onion, garlic, carrot, bell pepper, celery, potato, mushroom, sweet potato, winter squash, turnip or rutabaga, parsnip, broccoli, and brussels sprouts

1 to 2 cups (cooked) additional vegetables (greens will reduce in volume)—choose from: frozen peas; frozen corn; canned tomatoes (if you canned any over the summer, this is the perfect time to use them—they become warm reminders of the sun's power); canned or cooked beans; chopped kale, cabbage, mustard greens, turnip greens, broccoli rabe, or chard

Suggested seasonings:

Chopped fresh parsley

Pinches of dried herbs—choose from: thyme, rosemary, sage, basil, savory, marjoram, or a combination

Sea salt and freshly ground black pepper

1 tablespoon unbleached or whole wheat flour

$^1/_2$ to 1 cup vegetable broth

$^1/_2$ cup shredded cheese (optional)

Wholemeal Crust (page 173) or Classic No-Dairy Crust on page 77 (optional)

3 cups cooked mashed potatoes (optional)

Preheat the oven to 350°F.

In a large saucepan, heat the olive oil and add any combination of the diced vegetables. Sauté until tender—the cooked mixture should measure 2 to 3 cups.

To the sautéed vegetables add any or all of the additional vegetables—to measure 1 to 2 cups when cooked (remember, greens will reduce in volume). Cook briefly to wilt the greens and heat frozen ingredients through.

Season with parsley, dried herbs, and sea salt and pepper to taste.

Sprinkle the mixture with the flour. Stir well and simmer for a few minutes to allow the flour to cook, then add the vegetable broth, stirring until moist and thickened. At this stage, you may also add the cheese, if desired.

Place ingredients in a prepared round deep-dish pie plate. You may use a bottom crust, a top crust, or both (see Wholemeal Crust, page 173, or Classic No-Dairy

Crust, page 77; double each recipe for a two-crust pie)—or no crust at all.

If you decide to go crustless, top the pie with about 3 cups of cooked mashed potatoes (dotted with butter, if you like).

For the final touch, either cut a special symbol in the crust with a sharp knife or a cookie-cutter, or swirl one in the potatoes, using a spatula or spoon (suns and spirals are two great choices). Make your shape with gratitude in your heart for this good food and for the sun's return.

Bake your pie for 45 minutes, or until the crust is golden, and serve. (For a grand presentation, surround the pie on its serving platter with fresh evergreens.)

Plum Pudding

serves 6 to 8

Dark and rich as the winter earth, plum pudding is the perfect Yuletide dessert, reminiscent of Dickensian holidays and those more ancient still. This is a recipe to begin at dusk and come back to at dawn: You'll want to start preparing it a day ahead of time.

2 cups raisins
1 cup chopped prunes (the plums in plum pudding)
3/4 cup currants
1/2 cup sultanas or golden raisins
1 cup Guinness stout
1 cup unbleached white flour
1/2 cup firmly packed brown sugar
1/3 cup mixed candied citrus peel
1/4 cup finely chopped almonds
1/4 teaspoon freshly grated nutmeg
1/4 teaspoon cinnamon
1/4 teaspoon allspice
1/4 cup fine, dry bread crumbs
8 tablespoons butter or shortening
2 eggs, lightly beaten
Pinch of sea salt

In a ceramic bowl combine the raisins, prunes, currants, sultanas or golden raisins, and Guinness and allow the mixture to steep, covered, overnight. (You could do this as part of your Yule Eve ritual. Then, as you sit in your Power Place in the gathering darkness, you can think of these fruits resting quietly in the dark to become a part of your festive Yule celebration when the light returns.)

The next morning, after you greet the newly risen sun, place this Guinness-fruit mixture in a large bowl and combine with the flour, brown sugar, candied citrus peel, chopped almonds, nutmeg, cinnamon, and allspice.

In a smaller bowl, combine the bread crumbs, butter or shortening, eggs, and sea salt. Add this mixture to the ingredients in the large bowl and mix well.

Generously butter a $1^1/_2$-quart pudding mold or a heat-proof bowl. Spoon the batter into the mold and cover it with a lid or buttered aluminum foil tied onto the bowl with string.

Place a rack in a deep soup pot with enough hot water to come halfway up the sides of your mold when it's set on the rack. Steam the pudding for 2 to $2^1/_2$ hours. Allow it to cool until just warm, and unmold.

You may decorate and serve your plum pudding in so many magical ways:

- Splash it with warm brandy and light it with a match
- Cover it with a doily, sift powdered sugar over it, then remove the doily—instant snowy lace! Make a traditional hard sauce and enjoy the contrast of dark pudding and snowy sauce
- Surround or top your pudding with fresh greens; dried orange rounds, like little suns; clean rocks and stones (the earthy darkness of the pudding lends itself beautifully to honoring the element of earth—build a small cairn around it and top with a lighted candle to symbolize the sun's return from darkness); sprigs of holly; favorite holiday ornaments; or bare winter branches—or a grapevine wreath—laced with either gold ribbon or small lit tapers (be watchful).

Late-Winter Recipes

 ## Thousand-Names Bean Soup
serves 8 or more

They say the Goddess has a thousand names. This soup has a thousand beans (more or less). Think of each beautiful bean—with its perfect, smooth shell and striking speckles or variations in color—as a gift from the goddess in your soup pot. This substantial, hearty soup will warm you all the way through, even on the coldest, darkest day. And if you buy lots of different kinds of dried beans to mix for this recipe, the leftovers look interesting and attractive in glass jars. Tied with pretty ribbons, jars of mixed beans make great New Year's gifts. (It's supposed to be good luck to eat beans on New Year's Eve. And it's certainly good for you to eat them any time.)

3 cups dried mixed beans
3 tablespoons olive oil
1 large onion, chopped
3 to 4 garlic cloves
1 medium carrot, cut into $\frac{1}{2}$-inch chunks
1 celery stalk, tough strings removed, cut into $\frac{1}{2}$-inch chunks (optional)
8 cups vegetable broth (or more)
2 teaspoons sea salt

1 teaspoon dried herbs—choose one or more of the following: marjoram, sage, rosemary, thyme, savory, basil, and oregano
1 can tomatoes, chopped (optional)
1 or 2 chipotle peppers (optional)
Half-and-half (optional)

The night before you plan to make this soup, place the mixed dried beans in a large bowl. (You may purchase a bag of fancy beans already mixed, or invest in your own mix of different beans—dried beans are inexpensive.) Cover the beans with water and soak them overnight. (It can be fun to do this on a full-moon night—imagine your beans soaking up all that lunar energy.)

Next morning, drain off the bean water and you're ready to make your soup. If you forgot to soak your beans the night before, on the day of your soup-making, place the dried mixed beans in a large pot with enough water to cover them, and bring to a boil. Boil for 3 minutes (three is a magic number), then cover the pot, turn off the heat, and allow the beans to sit for 2 hours. Then proceed with the recipe.

In a very large soup pot, heat the olive oil. Add the onion, garlic, carrot, and celery and sauté until slightly softened.

Next add the vegetable broth, beans, sea salt, and the dried herbs of your choice. (Marjoram, sage, rosemary, or thyme are all delicious; savory is supposed to reduce the gassy effects of beans; basil and oregano, along with a can of chopped tomatoes added in the last $1/2$-hour of cooking, will give your soup a delightful Italian flavor. This recipe can be adjusted in infinite ways to suit your tastes. Toss in 1 or 2 chipotle peppers, if you like—they give a wonderful smoky taste as well as some additional heat.

Bring the soup to a boil, then reduce heat, cover, and simmer about 2 hours, or until the beans are tender, adding more broth, if necessary, to thin. Adjust the seasoning and serve hot—with crusty bread and a salad, you have a meal. (This soup may also be pureed in a blender. Remove the peppers, if you used them, and puree all or part of the soup, adding half-and-half, if desired, for an extra-creamy version.)

Rooted Winter Salads

Supermarkets offer a bounty of fresh greens even when the snow lies deep around us. Many of our ancestors weren't so lucky. Although they may have had an abundance of winter roots and legumes, their craving for crisp greens had to be satisfied with cooked cabbage or kale until spring. We can have the best of both worlds.

Crisp salad greens
Assorted vegetables—choose from:
  carrots, beets, potatoes, onions,
  turnips, parsnips, rutabagas, and
  sweet potatoes
Lively accents (optional): chopped
  nuts, raisins, cinnamon,
  Pomander Dressing (page 106),
  or freshly reamed orange or
  lemon juice

Choose a medley of your favorite vegetables to prepare simply.

Carrots and onions may be grated or minced raw—everything else may be lightly steamed, roasted, baked, or caramelized, or you could use leftover Heartha's Roasted Winter Vegetables (page 89).

On a bed of the freshest, crispest greens you can find, mound any or all of the warm vegetables to invite winter's grounded, earthy rootedness into your body and your home.

Winter salads often benefit from a touch of citrus, as well. Feel free to ream an orange or a lemon into your favorite salad dressing recipe to add a touch of Yuletide light and sparkle. Or you could use Pomander Dressing and add $1/4$ teaspoon ground cinnamon—root vegetables, citrus, and cinnamon cuddle up beautifully together in winter.

Top with a tablespoon of chopped nuts and raisins, if you like.

Winter Sunset Carrots

serves 4 to 6

Something about the bright, clear ginger taste of this recipe, coupled with the carrots' startling color, evokes winter sunsets and reminds us of the precious quality of light in this season. The days may be short, but the light is so beautiful.

2 tablespoons olive oil

3 to 4 cups carrots, scrubbed and cut into ¹/₂-inch rounds

1 to 2 tablespoons maple syrup, honey, or brown sugar

2 to 3 tablespoons freshly squeezed orange juice (or lemon juice, for a very zesty version)

2 teaspoons fresh minced ginger root (or 1 teaspoon dried powdered ginger, or 2 tablespoons crystallized ginger)

Sea salt

In a medium saucepan, heat the olive oil over medium-high heat. Sauté the carrots in heated oil until they are just crisp-tender. Then add the maple syrup, honey, or brown sugar along with the orange juice. Stir until the carrots are coated and the mixture has made a nice glaze.

Sprinkle with ginger (use more, if you like) and sea salt to taste. Stir to blend flavors and serve warm.

Leek and Potato Gratin

serves 4 to 6

Leeks and potatoes make delicious winter partners. This hearty classic is especially warming and soul-satisfying because it starts out white as the surrounding snow, but ends up as golden as the slowly strengthening sun.

2 cups low-fat milk

3 large potatoes, scrubbed and sliced into ¼-inch rounds

2 leeks, white parts only, washed well and sliced into ¼-inch rounds

1 garlic clove, minced or pressed

¼ teaspoon sea salt

1 cup shredded cheese (cheddar is usual, but you could try Gruyère, Jarlsberg, smoked Gouda, or Monterey Jack)

¼ cup grated Parmesan cheese

Preheat the oven to 375°F.

In a large heavy-bottomed or nonstick saucepan, combine the low-fat milk, potatoes, garlic, and sea salt to taste. Simmer over medium heat until the potatoes are fork-tender, about 20 minutes—be careful not to scorch them.

Using a slotted spoon, transfer the leeks and potatoes to a shallow baking dish, retaining the thickened hot milk in your saucepan.

Stir the cheese into the saucepan and continue stirring until the cheese is melted. This dish takes a bit of stirring—you could use this time to think of the snow that will begin to melt in just a little while, and the days that are gradually growing longer.

Pour the cheese-milk mixture over the leeks and potatoes in the baking dish. Sprinkle with the Parmesan cheese.

Bake until the gratin is bubbly and golden, about 30 minutes. Let your gratin cool for about 10 minutes before serving. (This dish is very pretty with a sprig of evergreen on top.)

Winter Fruit Pies

makes 4 individual pies or 1 large pie

Not that long ago, fresh fruit in winter was an unheard-of luxury for most people. But dried fruits, preserved at the height of summer with an eye toward the lean winter months ahead, can make delicious desserts with very little trouble. The late-winter goddess encourages us to experiment with different combinations, to see what will most please our eyes and palates. This final result is reminiscent of mincemeat pie, but is so much easier to make—and more healthful to eat.

2 **cups dried fruit, any combination—choose from: dried figs, prunes, apricots, peaches, pears, apples (all chopped), raisins, sultanas, currants, dried blueberries, cranberries, and cherries (all halved or left whole)**
²/₃ **cup brandy, rum, or whiskey**
¹/₃ **cup firmly packed brown sugar**
Juice of one lemon
2 **tablespoons butter or margarine**
1 **teaspoon vanilla extract**
¹/₂ **teaspoon cinnamon**
¹/₄ **teaspoon sea salt**
Wholemeal Crust (page 173) or Classic No-Dairy Crust on page 77 (optional)

To make the filling, place the dried fruit in a medium bowl—you can use any combination that pleases you (my current favorite is ¹/₂ cup each of apricots, peaches, currants, and raisins).

In a small saucepan, heat the alcohol, brown sugar, lemon juice, butter or margarine, vanilla extract, cinnamon, and sea salt. Stir over medium-high heat until this sauce bubbles and thickens slightly. Then, pour it over the fruit in the bowl, stirring to combine. Allow the fruit to steep in the sauce for at least 15 minutes.

Preheat the oven to 375°F.

Meanwhile, roll out the dough for your crust of choice. Wholemeal Crust or Classic No-Dairy Crust both work well—

double each recipe if you plan to make a top crust; or you could save time and use a packaged crust mix or a pre-made frozen crust.

Cut the dough to fit four individual $^1/_2$-cup tart tins. Press dough lightly into the tins, pinching the edges decoratively, if you wish. Spoon the fruit and sauce into the crusts. You may make lattice top crusts, or regular top crusts (slashed to allow steam to escape), or decorate the tops of the pies with little pastry leaves; or use no top crusts at all.

Bake pies for 35 minutes, if you used top crusts, or for 25 to 30 minutes, if your pies are bare (to avoid having the fruit become too browned)—or until the filling is bubbly and the crust is golden. Allow the pies to cool until just warm before serving.

soft breezes freshen the earth, and the world begins to flower. This is the season of renewal; if you need energy and inspiration, think of these magic words:

spring's watchwords New, tender, airy, revitalizing, tonic, flowering, lively, fresh, light

spring's scents and tastes Green onions, dill, vinegar, sweet flowers—hyacinth, lilac, lily of the valley, violet, rain-damp earth

Setting the Stage for Spring

*T*he *perfect spring house* is perched on a hill. Its eaves are steeped in clouds. Sky peers in through every window. The first rays of dawn turn the slate roof a warm, golden pink. Scores of birds nest in the gables; their lively singing in the morning and the freshness of the wind make it seem as if the house is flying. But that flight is anchored in the quickening earth.

All around the house are freshly dug garden beds, vivid with new shoots and leaves. Fruit trees incline toward the walls, branches starred with blossoms. Fallen petals drift across the door.

Inside, there is a sense of order and spaciousness. When you walk into the kitchen, you notice the clean, fresh feeling there. You stand in the middle of the room, taking a deep breath as you look around at the sunrise colors: pale rose, buttercup yellow, the tender blue of a wild bird's egg. Someone has polished the floor with loving attention. Someone has cleaned the countertops until they shine.

In the center of the scrubbed wooden table is a pot of flowering paperwhites. Their wild, sweet scent permeates the room. A nest sits nearby, filled with eggs decorated by hand—magical eggs with wishes in them.

The spring house is alive with a sense of the future. In it, plans, dreams, and inspirations can all be planted and nurtured. The door to the outer world is opening. As you look outside at the blossoming earth, your mind fills with hope.

The Spring Kitchen

Spring blossoms with festival days. On February 1, Imbolc, also known as Brigid's Day, is the first chilly harbinger of the season. Then, at spring's midpoint, we celebrate Ostara (or Eostre), the pagan festival of eggs and bunnies and new beginnings, from which the cultural Easter derives both its name and its imagery. Finally, May 1 is the pagan celebration of sex and fertility, a joyous affirmation of life.

Just like the season, spring kitchens are airy, fresh places where we feel stimulated, energized, alive with possibilities. The first step in making our kitchens places of inspiration is a good old-fashioned spring cleaning. Even those of us who loathe housecleaning as a tiresome, thankless, repetitious, and endlessly boring chore can learn to enjoy the process of marking our territory with magic. (See Cleaning, page 11, for some ideas on cleaning with magical consciousness.) When we realize that our cleaning work is making space for three magical celebrations in our homes and spirits, then we bypass the usual deadening "shoulds" around housecleaning in favor of anticipation—even a sense of liberation—instead.

By the end of winter, the world looks a bit scruffy and neglected. Dead leaves and fallen branches litter the ground, along with remnants of snow pocked with grime. Just as a gardener needs to clear away the winter debris to make room for spring growth and flowering, so it can be a good thing to clear away the debris from our kitchens. Make space in your life for fresh, good things to grow. Take some time in early spring to decide on your kitchen essentials. What is truly necessary for you? What could you do without? Give away anything that doesn't serve you. When your kitchen is clean and uncluttered, your spirit can breathe.

Once your kitchen is as clean as you feel like making it, you may want to celebrate the stirring of new life with a few essential springtime decorations. Flowering bulbs and bare tree branches can both be placed in water and allowed to bloom. Teardrops of glass hung in the window catch the light like melting icicles. Dark, earthy winter colors give way to the lighter, more airy ones of spring—a pastel rag rug for the floor or a woven mat for the table may refresh your spirit. Look for shades of mouthwatering yellow-green, violet, rose, pale blue, silvery dove-gray, and a tender yellow the color of the emerging sun. These are the colors that will help you to envision, to plan, to be inspired.

Spring is associated with air, and with thoughts, ideas, and words. You could invoke the power of words in your kitchen by writing a few important ones here and there. Use large letters if you want them to be seen (in a border around the ceiling, perhaps), or hide tiny ones in secret places. What are the words that you need in your life? Is there a special quote that you could frame or incorporate into your kitchen?

By Ostara, the Spring Equinox, the birds are returning and the world is filled with wings, nests, and the heart-lifting sound of their singing. One traditional and pleasant way to commemorate the birds' return is to include a nest or two in your kitchen. You could buy one (Spanish moss, twig, or wicker nests look very realistic), or you could find a real one (as long as it isn't being lived in anymore), or create your own. Although I have a preference for natural materials, you may want to try something completely different. One music-loving friend recycled some ruined audiotape for his spring offering— the shiny brown, curly tape made a perfect nest. And my kitchen Sheela-na-gig appears to enjoy her springtime perch inside an old chiffon scarf.

Fill your nests with eggs. Traditionally, eggs have held a place of special veneration as objects of power and magic. Egg decorating is an ancient way to honor this season (see Kitchen Rituals for Ostara, page 140, for some ideas). And you may want to tuck in a feather or two, as well—these are especially meaningful if you've found them yourself.

There are egg-shaped soaps available now that would be fun in a nestlike soap dish on the sink (look for all-natural herbal egg soaps in specialty stores or gift catalogs). Or, to make your own, grate leftover bits of soap into a bowl, mix with a little water, and shape small palmfuls into eggs by hand. If you throw in a few leftover coffee grounds, your soap will have a wild-bird speckled look and will also be a good deodorizer for oniony hands. Whenever you wash with a bar of egg soap, remind yourself of the incredible power to create that lies in your hands—and in your heart, your spirit, and your mind.

The first tender vegetables of the spring garden make a welcome appearance now. The garden's tiny carrots, cheery radishes, asparagus spears, and earliest peas may be found on everything from teapots to vases to dinnerware to tea towels, which will let you invite their hopeful message inside as well. Or you could paint or stencil the veggie of your choice somewhere special—inside a cupboard door to cheer you whenever you open it, for instance.

By late spring, the world is strewn with flowers. Make a place on your table for a vase spilling over with blooms, or find an O'Keeffe print to brighten your wall: The sensual beauty of flowers has age-old associations with love, sex, and pleasure, and late spring, with its Beltane celebration, is certainly the time for those. To invite the power of loving sensuality into your kitchen, choose fabrics and accents in shades of rose to remind you of your own sacred petals. Consider making a rose-patterned pillow for your Power Place; then, every time you sit there, you will be embowered by these rich symbols of the Goddess.

Spring Spell for Growing into Yourself

Join hands with the vibrant new energy of spring that encourages us to grow more fully into who we are, for the good of all. This fascinating, meditative spell takes some patience and willingness to experiment, but you will be amazed at the results you get. After all, there is power—and deep mystery—in names.

You will need:

> **A package of dried lima beans**
> **A permanent marker**
> **Paper and pencil**
> **A pot filled with soil**

First, pour out as many beans as there are letters in your name—your full name, including the middle one. Now mark each bean, putting one letter of your name on each one. This should give you plenty of letters to work with. Save the unmarked dried beans to make soup with later.

Now turn your attention to the letters of your name, laid out like Scrabble pieces in front of you. Begin to mix them around. What other words and names can you form with them? Take some real time to play and experiment, jotting down anything that feels right to you. There is often a special, mysterious surprise hidden in the letters of our names, keys to understanding something about our true selves. When I tried this, using my full name—Caitlyn Pamela Johnson—I found *Jolly Nan, Shamanic Poet.* (I haven't quite grown into it yet, but believe me, I'm working on it!) What secrets are hidden like seeds in the dark, fertile ground of your name?

When you have discovered your secret name, plant your beans in the soil. Water them generously and keep them warm. Watch how they sprout and grow into lush plants. If you have a garden, transplant them once the danger of frost is past. What does this process teach us about the time it takes to make things grow? Life is a process, filled with mystery and unexpected surprises. Happy spring!

Imbolc Magic

The Irish climate is milder than ours; to the ancient Celts, February 1 was the first day of spring. They called it Imbolc, from the words for "ewe's milk" or "in the belly" (sources differ on this), because pregnant sheep began to lactate at this time. Our Groundhog Day, with its anticipation of spring, is a leftover from the Celtic belief that magical animals come out of hibernation now.

Even in the frozen North, Imbolc can begin to show us the first signs of spring. The days are growing discernibly longer and there is a new energy in the air. More birds are singing, and a few hardy plants may even be showing their first shoots. But most of the activity happening now is underground. Imbolc celebrates not only the strengthening sun, but also the waking of the seeds that are beginning to stir in their dark winter beds.

Imbolc is devoted to Brigid, a fiery ancient Irish goddess of poetry, smithcraft, and healing. We need the fire of Brigid now, as an antidote to the blahs of endless gray days, endless cold, endless ice and dirty snow, and Brigid is all about

 the transformative power of fire: fire in the poet's mind, fire in the forge, fire in the healer's hands. Imbolc is the perfect day to write a poem, or to make a special craft (candle-making is traditional, as is the weaving of Brigid's Crosses out of wheat or rushes), or to perform hands-on healing for someone you love.

Kitchen Rituals for Imbolc

With six weeks or so of wintry weather still ahead of us, Imbolc rituals in the kitchen become an important affirmation that spring is happening, although most of the movement at this point is out of sight. Try bringing a handful of snow or ice indoors. Place it on the stove (fiery Brigid's favorite place in the kitchen) and watch it as it melts throughout the day. Know that the world will thaw soon.

You could also make a Threshold of Spring for your kitchen; its simple stone shapes echo the ancient Druid dolmens that were symbols of rebirth and renewal. In a pan or plate filled with dirt deep enough to anchor them, place two long rocks, standing up. Place a third rock across the tops of these standing stones—now you have made a threshold or gateway. Imbolc is such a threshold: Through it, we can see the first glimmering light of spring. Place a candle in the middle of your gateway to light at dusk.

Today is the perfect day to gather up and compost or burn any dry, dusty evergreens left over from the Winter Solstice, and to do a little spring cleaning (see Sue Bender's *Plain and Simple* for some inspiration; there are real spiritual benefits to getting all of your surfaces sparkling). If you're not up to doing the whole kitchen yet, you could do a microcosmic cleaning by dusting your kitchen altar; it counts. And since the oven, a source of fire, is sacred to Brigid, today would be a good time to clean it. Then you may want to light a white (or red-orange) candle inside it to invoke Brigid's presence there.

Spell for Movement and Change

There are times in every life when we feel stuck, when the ice of winter seems to catch in our hearts and movement of any kind becomes impossible. This spell is a heartening antidote. It may be performed at any time of the year, but it is particularly powerful at Imbolc, when nature's energies, just beginning to move after the long iced-over winter, can assist you.

You will need:

> **A piece of white paper**
> **A non-permanent-ink pen or marker**
> **A hole punch**
> **String or ribbon**
> **Water**
> **Your freezer**

On your piece of white paper, using the non-permanent-ink pen or marker, write down the areas where you feel you need movement and change—a relationship issue may come to mind, for instance, or a situation at work (very often, these areas include other people in them).

Fold or roll the paper into an icicle shape, punch a hole in one end, and tie a string through the hole. Now dip the paper in cold water and place it in the freezer. Take it out in a few hours, dip again, and refreeze. Continue until you have a sizable icicle with a heart of paper. Imagine that the ice sums up all the frozen patterns of behavior that have brought you to the present situation.

Suspend the icicle outdoors, where you can see it from a window in your home. As you hang the icicle, concentrate on the change or movement you need around the issue at hand.

You may want to say a short charm:

> *As you shift and change, so I will do—*
> *I will to change along with you.*

Now pay close attention to what happens to this icicle over time. Notice how it will thaw and melt one day, refreeze and grow rigid another. Give thought to your own ways of shifting and changing, then retreating into old patterns. It is a dance of ebb and flow.

When the ice has completely melted away, bring the remaining paper heart indoors and dry it out. Cut off the ribbon and carefully unroll the paper. How has your writing changed? You may find that the words have become art, the ink separating into pastel rainbows of color. You can keep this paper as a reminder of the ways we change—with consciousness and attention—over time, or you may want to offer it to Brigid by burning it in your fireplace or cauldron, scattering the ashes on your garden plot, if you have one, or in a potted plant.

> *All things shift and change at last:*
> *blessings on the dance.*
> *Blessings on the seeds we sow,*
> *blessings on the plants.*

Sprouting Meditation

Spring always seems to happen for the first time. Year after year, the endless weeks of winter cold seem to numb us, to make us forget. Deep inside ourselves, we begin to believe that it will always be like this—frozen, gray, dead. And then spring takes us by surprise. For uncounted centuries, people have paused to celebrate this seasonal miracle: Out of the seemingly barren earth comes new life. From tiny, dead-looking seeds the first sprouts grow, gladdening our hearts and nourishing our bodies with their cheerful green.

Sprouts are small emblems of courage and strength—triumphantly bursting out of their hard coffins, then blindly pushing their way up through dark soil to find the sun. Even if you live in a big city, you can experience this spring wonder right in your own home. Nothing is more amazing, if we take a little time to notice and to participate.

This is a three-day meditation, but it only takes a minute or two each day, and those minutes are spent in connection with the outrageously powerful life force that fuels and inspires this planet. If you just don't have the time to do the sprouting part of this meditation, then buy a box of sprouts at the store and skip directly to Embodying the Spring (page 131).

The Sprouting Experience

First, find a clean, widemouthed 1-quart jar.

Next, choose some dried, unhulled seeds or beans to sprout. My current favorites are sunflower seeds, but you could choose alfalfa, lentil, radish, garbanzo, wheat berries—or many other kinds. Just be sure that your seeds or beans aren't treated with any chemicals for planting; they should be intended for use as food.

Measure out about ¼ cup of your seeds or beans. Pour a few into your palm and really look at them. Roll them around with your fingers; really notice their texture. What a bizarre paradox they represent, these dried-up, rock-hard, dead little things, unassuming and uninspired. Do you sometimes feel like this at winter's end?

Now place your seeds in the jar. As you do, breathe a wish for the things you would like to come alive and grow in your life. What do you hope for in spring? How would you like to manifest your gifts? What qualities would you like to expand in the coming months?

Cover the seeds or beans with warmish water and allow them to soak overnight. Think of them whenever it occurs to you. They are softening in the water now, preparing to expand and break free of their winter prisons.

Next morning, cover the mouth of the jar with a clean nylon stocking or piece of cheesecloth (a rubber band will hold it in place) and turn the jar upside down to drain.

Cover the seeds or beans with water once or twice a day to moisten, draining off the water immediately each time. (You could give this sprout water to your houseplants; they need vitamins, too!) Each time you water your seeds, take a minute or two to notice how they are changing. Do you secretly think that this won't work, that your seeds will just sit there and mold? Do you have "sprouting anxiety" (telling yourself, "This may work for everyone else, but it won't work for me")? On the second or third day, look carefully and you will see that your seeds have split their casings. And then the first fine threads will emerge. After two or three days, your seeds *will* sprout!

Give them another day or two to grow. Then find a sunny place to put them for a few hours so they can turn a gorgeous spring green (just be careful to keep your sprouts on the cool side—otherwise they'll spoil). Once they're green and lush, take a minute to really savor their fresh color and lively energy. Then cover your sprouts and refrigerate them. Sprouts are best when used fresh, within just a few days.

Embodying the Spring

Take one of your sprouts with you to your Power Place. Sit and give it your full attention for a moment. Really notice the exact shade of its green. Does it remind you of anything? Does the color vary from one end to the other? How would you describe the stem? Is it tender, pale, vibrant? Straight or curly? Some sprouts are hairlike, while others are clearly the beginnings of small plants. How large are the leaves? How are they shaped?

Sniff your sprout thoughtfully. Sprouts often have a delicate sweet scent, like spring. Just think: This little miracle came from a tiny, dead-looking seed. Imagine all the ideas and projects that could sprout in you, if you encouraged them and consciously participated in the process. What would they be? What would you like to begin?

With these thoughts in mind, eat your sprout. Is it tender or crunchy? How does it taste? Some sprouts are slightly spicy or bitter, others are sweet. Imagine that this sprout will inspire you, helping you to envision wonderful new things this spring, season of new beginnings. Thank the sprout for its gifts.

Special Festival Recipe

Another way to honor Brigid's flame is by making the following special festival loaf. This recipe was given to me by my dear friend and sometime-coauthor Maura D. Shaw, who celebrates her Irish roots both in her writing and in the cooking she does for special occasions. This particular version of traditional Irish soda bread can trace its lineage back to the seaport of Dingle in County Kerry, Ireland, where it was baked over a peat fire.

Maura's Irish Soda Bread

makes 1 loaf

This cottage loaf has Imbolc magic in it. It is as round as the sun, is filled with sun-colored raisins, and has a sprinkling of caraway seeds to remind us of the seeds that are awakening now. There is something very satisfying about shaping this loaf by hand, an evocation of the days when bread was baked in a peat- or wood-fired oven dedicated to Brigid of the Flaming Hearth.

3½ cups unbleached flour
½ to ¾ cup raw or brown sugar
1 teaspoon baking powder
¼ teaspoon baking soda
1 stick butter, softened
1 egg
1¼ cups buttermilk (or regular milk soured with 1 teaspoon vinegar)
½ cup golden raisins or currants
1 teaspoon dried caraway seeds (optional)

Preheat the oven to 350°F.

In a large mixing bowl, combine the flour, raw or brown sugar (use more, if you like a sweet loaf), baking powder, and baking soda.

Cut the butter into the flour mixture until crumbly.

Add the egg and the buttermilk. Mix until moistened. The dough will be stiff. Add, working into the dough, the golden raisins or currants and the caraway seeds.

Form into a round loaf on a greased baking sheet. Use a knife to cut a spiral or other pattern into the top, if you wish; sunlike Brigid's Crosses are also traditional.

Bake for 1 hour.

Song of the Imbolc Goddess

Fire of dawn-light in her hair,

Fire flows like milk from her hands.

Fire of bright promise in her springing step,

Fire of the flame in her eyes.

A blessing on your hearthfire,

On your gift of words,

On the brightness of your sacred body,

A blessing on your flame.

Early-Spring Recipes

Brigid's Broth of Inspiration

serves 4 to 6

By the beginning of February, many of us, weary of the unending cold and gray, find ourselves suffering from full-blown winter blahs. Imbolc's ancient associations with the first day of spring are tantalizing, but we know we still have a full month (or more) of cold weather ahead of us. The vista is unappealing. How can we imagine new projects when we feel so low? How can we energize ourselves when we still feel so stuck?

Well, take heart. Irish Brigid (or Bridget, or Brigit, or Bride), the redheaded and fiery goddess of inspiration and healing (among other things), can give us what we need to break out of our hard, dry winter shells. Make her delicious, spicy soup as a wake-up call to your own inner self: The ingredients will give you the courage to face the demands of spring with renewed zest and vigor.

Before you begin, you may want to invoke Brigid by lighting a small candle near your chopping board. Its warm flame will remind you of her sacred fire.

And you could remember—or say or sing—the following song to Brigid, by friend and priestess Elizabeth Cunningham:

> *Brigid, red-gold woman,*
> *Brigid, flame and honeycomb—*
> *You are my bright, precious freedom.*
> *Brigid, lead me home.*

2 tablespoons olive oil	1 medium carrot, diced
3 leeks, white parts only, washed well and cut into 1/2-inch rounds	2 teaspoon paprika
	1/4 teaspoon cayenne
1 red bell pepper, diced	6 cups vegetable broth or water

Sea salt
Handful of garlic-mustard greens,
coarsely chopped
1 to 2 cups croutons
4 to 6 dollops sour cream
Sprouts for garnish

In a large soup pot, heat the olive oil. Add the leeks, red pepper, and carrot and heat, stirring occasionally, until barely tender. Sprinkle vegetables with paprika and cayenne to taste. As you sprinkle, visualize Brigid's fiery energy filling the pot; the cheery orange-red color is a warming reminder of her vivid hair and of the sun that is slowly bringing the frozen earth back to life.

Cover the vegetables with the vegetable broth or water and sea salt to taste. Bring to a boil and cook, covered, for 15 minutes.

Add the handful of garlic-mustard greens. (Use a field guide and search your own yard, if possible—garlic mustard is usually up and growing, even at this chilly time of year). If garlic mustard is unavailable, substitute parsley or watercress. As you stir these into the broth, think of the green of the new plants just beginning to sprout and grow outdoors. This same green vitality is now a part of your soup.

Continue cooking for 2 or 3 minutes.

Place several croutons into individual bowls, ladle soup into the bowls, and top each serving with a dollop of sour cream.

Arrange two or three of the sprouts from your Sprouting Meditation (page 129) on the sour cream. There you have it: a broth as fiery as Brigid's hair, topped with sprouts emerging from the snow— a warming and reviving homage to spring's return.

Sprouted Spring Salads

Add some spring vitality to your salads with the sprouts you grew for your Sprouting Meditation—or try some of the sprouted offerings at your local grocery or natural foods store. Any or all of the following sprouts make great additions to your salad bowl:

adzuki • alfalfa • barley • garbanzo • lentil • mung • oat • radish • soy • sunflower • wheat berry

You may want to dip mung or other sprouted beans in hot or boiling water for a few seconds before rinsing with cold water and adding to your salad. Soybeans need to be boiled for 5 minutes to remove harmful enzymes. (All sprouts contain some saponins, but these are not toxic unless eaten in huge quantities—moderation is the key.)

Spring Greens

serves 4 to 6

Next time you're at the grocery store or the local produce market, notice how many different kinds of greens there are. What will you choose for this quintessential spring food? You could use the tender tops of radishes or turnips that many people just throw away, or the succulent leaves of new beets. Spinach, collards, watercress, mustard greens, and bok choy will all work well, too. Or you could forage in your backyard for some early dandelions. You may combine several greens for this recipe, or stick to just one. Either way, you are eating the Earth's green energy when you make this dish in spring.

6 to 8 cups packed greens
  Sea salt, tamari, or shoyu to taste
  1 tablespoon chopped scallion or green onion (optional)

Bring a large pot of water to a boil.

Using a steamer basket, steam the greens for a few minutes until just tender.

Sprinkle each serving with the sea salt, tamari, or shoyu to taste and the chopped scallions or green onion, if you like.

Magic Isle Pasties

serves 4

Pasties are main-dish turnovers, like little portable potpies. They are popular in many places—throughout the British Isles, and in the Upper Peninsula of Michigan (where I was introduced to them). This delicious vegan version is warming, nourishing, and filled with a foretaste of spring—the perfect Imbolc offering. And like so many of the recipes in this book, the ingredients may certainly be varied according to your tastes and the contents of your pantry or fridge.

Classic No-Dairy Crust (page 77) or piecrust dough of your choice (enough for two crusts)

2	**tablespoons butter or olive oil**
1	**onion, diced**
2	**cups cabbage, chopped**
1	**medium potato, diced**
1	**carrot, diced**
1/2	**green pepper, diced**
1/4 to 1	**cup vegetable broth (amount needed will vary)**
1/2	**cup chopped wild greens, water cress, or parsley**
3	**green onions, chopped**

Pinches of herbs—choose from: savory, dill, thyme, sage, or whatever sounds good to you

Sea salt and freshly ground black pepper

Preheat the oven to 375°F.

In a large saucepan, heat the butter or olive oil. Add the onion, cabbage, potato, carrot, and green pepper and stir frequently, until vegetables are softened. Moisten the vegetables with a little broth.

When vegetables are tender, add the wild greens, watercress, or parsley; green onions; herbs; and sea salt and pepper to taste.

Make the Classic No-Dairy Crust, or your favorite piecrust recipe, enough for a double crust. Divide dough into four balls and roll out to form ovals approximately 8 inches by 5 inches. Heap each oval with about 1/2 cup of the vegetable mixture, then fold the long end over and crimp the edges together. If you have any leftover filling, bake it in a dish alongside your pasties, or save it to use in soups, stews, or scrambled eggs.

Place pasties on a baking sheet and bake 30 to 40 minutes, or until the pastry is golden. May be served hot or warm.

Waking Earth Cake

serves 6 to 8

This unusual cake is an adaptation of a recipe from Harriet Kofalk's *The Peaceful Cook*. When you read the (very short) list of ingredients, you may wonder how anything this simple could taste good. The cake contains no salt, no vanilla, no butter or eggs, but it *is* good—and molasses offers us a nourishing tonic for the last cold days of early spring.

If you include a special surprise or two in with your batter (see list of ingredients) you can experience a true Imbolc delight: This tasty cake (that looks so like the slumbering earth) is hiding a wonderful gift, just as the earth is gestating the waking seeds and the first stirrings of spring.

1½ **cups whole wheat flour**
1 **cup unbleached white flour**
1½ **teaspoons baking soda**
½ **cup vegetable oil**
½ **cup unsulphured molasses**
½ **cup hot water**
¼ **cup blackstrap molasses**
Surprises—non-meltable!—
  for hiding inside cake (optional):
  a clean coin, a small polished
  crystal, a ring, a small gold
  or silver charm
Yogurt or ice cream (optional)

Preheat the oven to 375°F.

In a large bowl, combine both flours and baking soda. Stir in the vegetable oil and the unsulphured molasses. This mixture will resemble crumb topping. Remove 1 cup of it and reserve.

In a small bowl, combine the hot water and the blackstrap molasses. Add to the flour mixture in the large bowl and mix well.

Now is the time, if you desire, to stir in any one or more of the non-meltable surprises. Finding one of them in your piece of cake is good luck—but be sure to warn your eating audience, to prevent accidental choking or broken teeth!

Pour batter into a buttered 9-inch square baking pan, sprinkle with the reserved crumb topping, and bake for 30 minutes, or until a toothpick inserted in the center comes out clean.

Serve warm, with a dollop of yogurt or ice cream, if you like. (Vanilla ice cream works beautifully to represent the snow covering this waking earth.) You could also top this cake with lit candles, one for each person who will be enjoying it.

Ostara Magic

*T*he *Spring Equinox, which occurs between March 20 and 23,* marks a moment of perfect balance between night and day—but after this, the days will be longer than the nights. Imbolc was the threshold to spring; now Ostara grabs our hands and pulls us through, leading us joyously into the growing time of year. Many early western Europeans called this festival Eostre, named after a Saxon goddess of spring—which is where the Easter holiday gets its name. It is a celebration of the earth's resurrection, the return of life and growth and fertility to the world.

Ostara is such a brave and tender time. As the first bulbs begin to flower, regardless of the chill, and new chicks and other creatures are born in the teeth of cold winds and voracious predators, we turn our attention to both the fragility and the dauntless courage of new life. It takes a lot of energy to break out of the egg. Ostara activities are designed to encourage and enliven us to do just that—to break out of the shell of hibernation or old, stuck

 patterns and embrace the new vistas waiting for us on the other side. The egg becomes our central emblem.

Even the cultural Easter holiday celebrates the egg—as well as all the other ancient goddess tokens of fertility and birth: flowers, nests, grass, baby bunnies, chicks. But eggs are central—we are practically bombarded with them, hard-boiled and confectionery, real and plastic. It can be illuminating to think of the ways in which our ancestors revered the egg as a source of life and a symbol of the Goddess, and to give some thought to the new things we wish to grow and nurture in the months ahead.

Kitchen Rituals for Ostara

Egg-dyeing becomes the perfect kitchen ritual activity for Ostara. There are commercial egg-dyeing kits in every grocery store. Or you might like to try doing it the old-fashioned way (*Celebrating the Great Mother* has a section on coloring eggs with food—onion skins, red cabbage, and beets). One year I bought a pysanky-making kit and spent several very satisfying hours decorating eggs with beeswax and brilliantly colored dyes. Pysanky are an old Ukrainian tradition; making them was once a magical rite. Look in your local craft shop to find a kit. As you color your eggs, give some thought to the projects, plans, and dreams that you would like to incubate.

In this season of new beginnings, you could perk yourself up by trying something new in the kitchen: a new food (I tried ume plum vinegar for the first time in the spring and loved it—this unusual ingredient makes a special appearance in several of the following Mid-Spring Recipes), a new cooking gadget, a new recipe. We all tend to get stuck in the same old boring routines—some inspiring spring newness may be just what you need to shake off the last of the winter blahs.

In our kitchen, we have a flat wicker basket for winter hats and mittens. The day we put the basket away is a ritual celebration of winter's end and the true arrival of spring. What sort of kitchen winter-to-spring ritual could you invent for yourself? Allow the spring winds of creativity to inspire you.

Because spring is associated with air, today would be a good day to light some dried

sage and allow your kitchen to be purified by the sacred smoke. Then sit in your Power Place and write lists, make plans, and begin imagining a healthier, more joyful future for yourself, your family, and the planet.

Spell for Incubating Your Secret Longing

The first step toward attaining your heart's desire is to really long for it. How often do we even allow ourselves to want anything? Many of us go on for years taking care of everyone else's needs without admitting we have any of our own. So on Ostara, allow yourself to focus on what you really, truly, deeply need. Most of us have the same, very basic longings: to love and to be loved, to be seen and heard, to be appreciated, to have a venue for our gifts, to have those gifts received by others, to feel connected. What is the nature of your secret longing?

It often takes a space of time, like the gestation period in the egg, before the universe responds to you. But respond it will. First, you have to have the courage to long for what you really want.

You will need:

> **A raw egg**
> **A piece of paper and pen**
> **A small crystal or other sacred object**
> **Glue**
> **Colorful tissue paper**

Take the raw egg and cradle it in your hand. Eggs are possibilities. Feel an Ostara sense of your own possibilities. Now gently allow yourself to name your heart's secret longing. Really long for it, feel your yearning. Write your longing on a small piece of paper and fold it up. Breathe on it.

Now crack open your egg carefully and put the contents aside to cook and eat later. Inside the pieces of shell (it will help if you've cracked it cleanly and there are only two pieces to deal with) place the folded paper and the small crystal or other

 sacred object. Glue the shell back together, then wrap it with colorful tissue paper. Keep it in a safe place, visiting it occasionally to warm it in your hands, giving yourself time (and permission) to feel your longing. Prepare to be amazed at the ways in which the universe will give to you.

Hatching Meditation

This meditation, while beautifully appropriate for the Ostara season, is useful anytime you need to expand beyond the boundaries of the familiar. Stretching beyond our current limits is sometimes painful, but it seems to be the necessary prerequisite for attaining our heart's true desire. Many blessings on your own hatching and growing.

Find a time when you can be alone and undisturbed. Sit comfortably with your eyes closed. Listen to the sounds around you; become gently aware of the small noises that make up your world at this moment. Now bring your attention to the sound of your own breathing, the rhythm it makes as it enters and leaves your body. Together, these are the sounds your world makes.

Next, imagine that you are sitting inside a large egg. Imagine the smooth, curving wall, the gentle darkness, the way the egg fits you perfectly, enclosing you in a small universe. It is quiet and safe—the only world you have ever known, the only one you've ever seen. But you are growing. The eggshell is gradually becoming cramped and close. You become aware of an urgent desire to stretch, to expand. The walls are hard and thick. But you are impelled—through some mysterious force of soul—to push . . . to push hard. You need space to grow. The wall cracks. You push harder still. Perhaps you kick or hit the walls with your fists. Soon the wall begins to break open and you push your way out. The shell is sharp and scratchy; it can hurt to break out of the egg. But you struggle—and suddenly there is a vast, enormous vista before you, a world you never dreamed of, a spaciousness you never imagined possible. Look around at this huge expanse. There is unlimited room and potential for growth. Stretch yourself as fully as you can. Really allow yourself to feel the exhaltation of breaking free into something larger than the familiar. Take a deep breath and open your eyes.

Song of the Ostara Goddess

Crowned with sweet tulips, with snowdrops and lilies,

She gathers the nests in her arms.

She broods over eggs, she shelters small creatures.

The shape of her body burns bright in the grass.

All around you, the smallest ones hatch,

Then they fly and they sing.

Take heart, take heart and take wing.

Mid-Spring Recipes

Ukemochi Miso Soup
serves 4

The first fragile blossoms of spring always remind me of exquisite Japanese prints. When we make this delicate and delicious soup, we share the Japanese appreciation of spring's beauty as we honor the Japanese goddess Ukemochi.

Ukemochi is a goddess of food, all food: Everything we eat came from her body. This soup makes use of miso, a protein-rich, concentrated paste made from fermented soybeans (according to tradition, soybeans sprouted from Ukemochi's womb). Miso is a staple of Japanese cooking—look for it in the refrigerator section of your local natural foods store.

This recipe is simplicity itself, but it may be varied in so many ways. Although the paler varieties of miso are the sweetest, you could try using a darker type for a heartier taste. Or you might try boiling a few vegetables—onions, potatoes, carrots, zucchini—in the hot water before adding the miso. Simmer some mushrooms in the soup for a couple of minutes; throw in a handful of chopped greens or soaked dried seaweed (wakame or kombu is delicious); or sprinkle in a little dry sherry, toasted sesame oil, or ume plum vinegar. Some cubed firm tofu would add interesting texture and extra protein. Let your Spring cravings be your guides.

4 cups water
1/2 cup yellow miso
1 tablespoon tamari or shoyu
1 tablespoon green onion, thinly sliced, for garnish (optional)

In a saucepan, heat the water.

Place 1/2 cup of the hot water in a small mixing bowl and add the miso, stirring to dissolve.

Stir the miso mixture into the remaining hot water in the soup pot and mix well, making sure not to boil. (Boiling destroys beneficial organisms; miso, like yogurt, is rich with them.)

Add the tamari or shoyu; mix well.

Ladle the soup into bowls and top each serving with green onion, if you like.

Salad Nests

serves 1

This salad is a pretty reminder of returning birds and nesting activity everywhere.

Alfalfa sprouts (1 generous handful for each serving)
1 tablespoon scallions, finely chopped (per serving)
Whole, blanched almonds
Ume Plum Dressing (recipe follows)

For each serving, take a generous handful of alfalfa sprouts and gently form the sprouts into a nestlike shape.

Fill each nest with about 1 tablespoon of scallions. Top with several almonds (these look charmingly egglike).

Drizzle each nest with Ume Plum Dressing.

Ume Plum Dressing

serves 4

Japanese ume plum vinegar gives a delicate pink color, piquant salty flavor, and delicious fruity, flowery bouquet to this exceptional dressing. Look for it at your local natural foods store; it's worth every penny.

¹/₃ cup olive oil
2 tablespoons ume (or umeboshi) plum vinegar

Combine the olive oil and plum vinegar in a jar with a tightly fitting lid. Put the lid on the jar and shake until dressing is smooth.

New Potatoes with Dill

serves 4

New potatoes are a springtime tradition. The visual appeal of their lovely pinkish color and egglike shape, as well as their overall deliciousness, make their appearance in our mid-spring meals most welcome.

2 pounds small red new potatoes
2 tablespoons olive oil
Sea salt
2 tablespoons snipped fresh dill

Preheat the oven to 350°F.

Place the potatoes in an 8-inch square baking dish. Drizzle with half of the olive oil and toss potatoes to coat.

Sprinkle with sea salt to taste and drizzle again with the remaining olive oil.

Bake, stirring once or twice to ensure even cooking, until potatoes are tender inside and crisp outside—about $1\frac{1}{2}$ hours.

Remove the potatoes from the oven and sprinkle with the dill. Serve hot.

Spring Supper Omelet with Mushrooms

serves 4

Eggs have been revered as magical symbols and talismans of power for millennia. Virtually every ancient or indigenous culture has made use of the sacred egg—for healing, protection, fertility magic, divination, spell-casting, and more.

As you crack the eggs for this dish, really notice how each yolk mimics the sun. Think of the wonder of eggs that contain new life inside their rigid, dead-looking shells. Give a moment or two to honor your own body's eggs, the perfection of their roundness like small moons, the miraculous journey they make (or used to make) inside your body. Honor the Great Mother's ability to make new life. It is good to celebrate eggs.

2 tablespoons olive oil
1 cup mushrooms, preferably wild*
4 green onions, chopped
2 cloves garlic, minced
Splash of:
    tamari or shoyu,
    ume plum vinegar, and
    toasted sesame oil
6 eggs
Sea salt and freshly ground
    black pepper
Fresh parsley or watercress sprigs
    for garnish

In a large frying pan with a lid and a metal handle, heat the olive oil. Add the mushrooms, stirring frequently until softened.

Sprinkle the mushrooms with the green onions and chopped garlic. Add a splash (if desired) of tamari or shoyu, ume plum vinegar, and toasted sesame oil.

In a small bowl, lightly beat together the eggs, sea salt, and pepper.

Distribute the vegetables evenly in the pan and pour in the eggs. Lower heat, cover the pan, and cook the eggs until they are completely set. Finish the omelet in the broiler for a few minutes to brown the top, if desired.

Loosen the omelet by sliding a spatula underneath it. Turn out onto a platter, cut in wedges, and serve. Garnish each serving with sprigs of fresh parsley or watercress.

*Wild mushrooms are gradually becoming available in grocery stores and markets. But if your store doesn't carry them, substitute the usual kind. Do not try to pick your own unless you're sure you know what you're doing.

 # Maple Candy
makes about 1 pound

In New England, maple sugaring time falls near the Spring Equinox, when the sap begins to move in the trees, bringing them back to life. If you live near a maple syrup farm, consider visiting. When you see the buckets filling, you become a witness to this otherwise invisible mystery.

Real maple syrup isn't cheap, but it is well worth the price. It is a uniquely American taste of springtime. Europeans were introduced to this New World treat by Native

Americans, who had been making maple syrup for many, many springs. Maple syrup is a treat we can feel good about—harvesting it doesn't harm the trees and it's a bit healthier for us than refined sugar.

This recipe can be a once-a-year splurge. The process is fascinating, and the result is sheer sensual delight—creamy, sweet, like eating concentrated tree energy.

Seasonal Easter-candy molds offer an opportunity for fun, and when we realize that bunnies and eggs are fertility symbols sacred to the Goddess, their use takes on an entirely new dimension. (Even Easter lilies have a hidden goddess story: They were once sacred icons of the Goddess's vulva. Perhaps it isn't so strange that many Sheela-na-gigs are found in churches.)

2 cups real maple syrup

Using a candy thermometer, in a sturdy saucepan with high sides, bring the maple syrup to a boil.

Turn heat to very low and allow syrup to continue boiling without stirring until the thermometer reads 233°F. Be careful that the syrup doesn't boil over—once maple syrup finally decides to boil, it really boils. The boiling action is mesmerizing; the syrup's dark earthy color in such constant motion reminds us that the earth itself is constantly moving and changing, even when it appears to remain the same.

When the reduced syrup has reached 233°F, remove it from the heat and allow to cool, still without stirring it, until the thermometer reads 110°F.

Now it's time to beat the reduced syrup with a wooden spoon. Beat vigorously for several minutes. (It can help to sing while you do this.) You are making a transformation take place: As you beat, the syrup gradually turns a pale caramel color and it becomes stiff enough to hold a shape.

Place in candy molds or form into patties on a plate or baking sheet and allow to cool completely.

Unmold and enjoy.

Handmade Spring Chocolates

If maple isn't your thing, you could make these very easy chocolates in any of the shapes of the season.

Good-quality chocolate (semisweet, bittersweet, or milk chocolate)
Melted butter (optional)
Cream (optional)

Simply melt the chocolate (I like mine bittersweet) in a double boiler and then place the melted chocolate in molds. If you like slightly softer chocolate candies, add a little melted butter and cream to the chocolate, stirring to mix.

Allow to cool completely, then unmold and enjoy.

Beltane Magic

It can be hard not to think about sex in the Spring—everything seems to be doing it. Our ancestors had a special festival on May 1 to honor sensual pleasure and the reproduction that is so often its end result—because without sex, there would be no life. This special day was called Beltane and it celebrated the amazing fecundity of the Earth and everything that lives upon her.

Beltane is unashamedly joyous and erotic. Whether we are with a sexual partner or not, there is great exuberance in being fully embodied, in pleasing that body with loving touch and delicious food. Dancing the Maypole, jumping the bonfire, crowning each other with blossoms, bringing the May sweetness indoors to deck our homes—all of these traditional ways of honoring Beltane are, above all, invitations to praise the body and Earth with pleasure, to fall in love with this glorious planet at this glorious time of year.

Kitchen Rituals for Beltane

Beltane is the time of blooming—your kitchen goddess may appreciate a flower on her altar today. Many of our ancestors placed representations of sex organs on their altars at Beltane; a red flower will celebrate the female, or you could make a vulva out of clay or paint one on paper. If you want to include a male organ, appropriately shaped rocks (sometimes called lingams) could be used—or you could make something more graphic out of clay. If you have a partner of the opposite sex, the more subtle among you could use a bell (male clapper inside female shell) to symbolize the union of the sexes. Those who are more overt could find, draw, or make something visibly erotic.

If you ever thought about making love in the kitchen (with a partner or by yourself), today is definitely the day. You will never look at your kitchen floor (or table or countertop) the same way again.

But the best way to honor Beltane in our kitchens is by cooking sensual foods. Whether we live alone or with a loving partner, whether we are sexually active or celibate, we all have bodies—and our wise bodies, with their incredibly complex world of nerve endings and processes, have such an amazing capacity for enjoyment. When we give ourselves foods rich in taste, texture, and visual beauty to feast upon, we feed our spirits and we honor the gifts of Earth.

Spells for Attractiveness

What is the secret of attraction? We all know people who are not in any sense conventionally beautiful, but we find ourselves drawn to them by something we can't define. I think it's all about goddess-nature: When we allow it to shine through us, we become irresistible. The following spell ideas (some new, some very old) encourage and facilitate this. When your own natural inner radiance, sensuality, and goddess-juiciness come shining through, who could possibly resist you? (These spells do *not* fall into the category of coercing someone specific into falling for you—which is definitely not all right and usually comes back in various nasty ways to haunt the perpetrator. Instead

 they focus on calling forth your own unique goddess-beauty and loveliness.) So, for Beltane, try a few of these and see what happens!

1. As you gaze into a mirror, repeat, "I am a channel for the Goddess. She needs me to be strong and authentic. The more I am true to myself, the more I am true to her." Imagine beginning to hold yourself like a Goddess, walk like a Goddess. Allow a Goddess-like sense of dignity and utter lovableness to permeate your very being.

2. Nothing is more powerfully attractive to others than the feeling that they are really being heard by you. The charm of someone who truly listens is undeniable. Anoint your ears with oil of lavender to help you open them to others.

3. Dust your underthings with powdered orrisroot. This dried root of the iris flower was used in this way for centuries—before the advent of underwear, women used it on the garments closest to their skin. Think of it as fairy dust helping you to rise above your usual way of relating.

4. Chew cloves. They're a bit spicy, they're delicious, they sweeten your breath. And when you taste the heat on your tongue, remember your own fiery nature and revel in it! Attraction is partly about electricity, about fire and heat. Cloves help you amp it up.

5. Draw a partnership rune (Gyfu, shaped like an X, is good) on your inner thigh with red lip liner or something else that makes a nontoxic red coloring (geranium petals work, and so does raw beet juice.) Just like sexy underwear, even if no one else can see it, you know it's there—and a sense of its mystery and allure will show on your face.

6. Hair has centuries-old associations with attraction. Mer sirens called hapless sailors to them by combing their hair. As you brush yours, visualize infusing each strand with the electric power of fascination. Tie a small piece of hair with red thread where it will not show, if possible. Touch this thread whenever you need to remind yourself of your electric fire.

Flower Meditation

Flowers are the sexual parts of plants. They are frankly and unabashedly sensual, their shapes, colors, and scents designed to attract the insects that will pollinate them. We can enter into the spirit of the great Beltane celebration by really spending time with a flower. It's all right there.

Choose a time when you can be quiet and undisturbed—preferably outdoors, if the weather permits. Find a flower to appreciate, one growing in your yard, if possible (violets are often blooming around Beltane and are perfect for this meditation because they are edible.) You may need to take a little Beltane stroll to find your blossom, if nothing appears nearby.

Pick the flower you've found and sit comfortably with it. As you begin to notice its colors and shapes, gently bring your attention to your breathing, its dance, its in-and-out pattern. As you grow quieter, focus fully on the blossom, on the shade and shape of its petals. How do its petals remind you of your own? Touch the flower gently—petal textures vary, but most are indescribably soft and delicate. Explore the curves of the petals, the strength and pliancy of the stalk. If you twirl the flower in your hand, it may look like a ballerina's skirt. Notice that your flower may have one or more stamens—those virile male parts—half-hidden in the folds of its petals. Notice their erect vitality, and the pollen that subtly coats your finger if you touch one, like the dust from a butterfly's wing. Smell your flower. Does it have a scent? How would you describe it?

Nature is almost unbearably erotic; allow yourself to fully enjoy the sensual pleasure of your flower. If it is edible, you may want to complete this meditation by taking the blossom into your mouth and tasting its complex flavor. Return what remains to the earth, and thank the flower for its fragile, delicious beauty. Nonedible flowers may be taken indoors and kept in water for a few, brief days, as a reminder of all the sensual Beltane activity—all the business of life—going on around us. We are a part of it, too.

Song of the Beltane Goddess

Lush is her body in the morning light

And drenched with dew, her blossoms.

Stretched open to sun on green, green grass,

She beckons us, calls us by name.

If you open to me I will feed you,

And all I ask is your love,

Your love for this earth ripe with beauty,

Your love for the hunger I feed.

Late-Spring Recipes

 ## Sensuous Spinach Soup *serves 4 to 6*

This simple, delicious, and pretty bright green soup has a sensuous texture that most of us associate with butter and cream—but this vegan recipe achieves the creaminess without fat and with a minimum of preparation, so there's more time to stroll around picking wild greens for the Wild Salad (page 156).

6 cups water or vegetable broth
1 large onion, coarsely chopped
3 potatoes, cut into chunks
1 tablespoon tamari
4 cups tightly packed fresh spinach
2 teaspoons dried basil
Freshly ground black pepper
Sea salt
Garnishes (optional):
    Carrot
    Hard-boiled egg
    Ground coriander

In a large soup pot, place the water or vegetable broth, chopped onion, potatoes, and tamari. Bring to a boil, then reduce heat, cover, and simmer for 35 minutes.

Add the spinach, basil (a great love herb), and pepper to taste. Cook for another 2 minutes, to wilt the spinach.

Remove from heat, and puree the soup in batches in a blender. Add sea salt to taste and serve.

If you've made this soup for a love partner (actual or potential), you may want to garnish with a traditional aphrodisiac. Try either a curl of carrot (use your vegetable peeler) or a slice of hard-boiled egg, with or without a sprinkling of ground coriander on top.

Wild Salad

On a warm spring day, the call of the outdoors is irresistible. Why fight it? Find some free time, grab a gathering basket and a good field guide to weeds, and head outside. You are about to experience the ancient pleasure of food gathering. There is no fresher or more healthful food than that which we pick ourselves, and the act of finding and gathering it gives us a bone-deep feeling of satisfaction, a direct link with our gatherer ancestors.

But first, a few cautions:
- Be sure any yard or wild area you harvest from is free from pesticides and other harmful chemicals.
- Make sure anything you pick is at least three feet from the road or highway (anything too close to the street will be contaminated by car exhaust).
- Avoid areas frequented by dogs, or places where you see deer droppings.
- Refer to your field guide—you'll want to be sure you know what you're picking.

With those warnings out of the way, take a moment to breathe deeply. Close your eyes and lift your face to the sun. Feel the warmth on your closed eyelids. Become aware of your feet, resting firmly on the earth. Now open your eyes. As you look around, know that you are surrounded by an amazing treasure trove of delicious green food. It isn't wrapped in plastic. It doesn't cost a thing. The Earth Mother offers it to you for free, because you are her child.

Become a treasure seeker—the greens and weeds around you are filled with healing. Begin to wander, looking here and there. When you find something good, pick a little of it and pop it in your basket. Soon, your rhythms will slow, your mind will grow quiet, and at the end of a pleasant ramble in the sun you will have a salad bursting with nourishment and wild goodness.

Wild Greens—you may find:
  Chickweed
  **Dandelion (both the tender leaves
    and blossoms)**
  Dock (curly and other varieties)
  Garlic mustard
  Lamb's-quarters
  Plantain
  Purslane
  Red clover
  Sheep sorrel
  Winter cress or rocket
  Wood sorrel
  Violet (both leaves and blossoms)
    Caution: **Pick only if you see its
    purple flowers; there are a few
    toxic plants with similar heart-
    shaped leaves.**

Olive oil
**Vinegar or freshly squeezed lemon
  juice**

Head home when you have enough for the people you are feeding. Wash the greens by dunking them briefly in a sink full of cold water, then pat them dry with a clean towel.

Toss your greens in a bowl with just a little olive oil and a few drops of good vinegar or freshly squeezed lemon juice. Sprinkle the top with some of the dandelion or violet flowers you found, and serve.

As you savor each tender, delicious mouthful, thank the Great Mother for your Wild Salad experience.

Beltane Asparagus

serves 4

Fresh asparagus is one of the true pleasures of spring. These green delights, reminiscent of the male sexual organ, have been prized for centuries as an aphrodisiac. Asparagus has its place in ancient ritual, as well—ancient Greek Maenads rigged up great phallic wands with asparagus-like tips in honor of the power of fertilization.

This Beltane recipe pairs the masculine and the feminine, partnering asparagus with almonds (our ancestors recognized the almond's vulva shape). This savory method of roasting the almonds comes from my friend Pangea, whose exquisite pottery and delicious food are always an inspiration.

1 **pound fresh asparagus spears**
2 **tablespoons butter**
  (optional)
Toasted Tamari Almonds
  (recipe follows)

Wash the asparagus and prepare by snapping off the bottom of each spear. It will break off with a satisfying crack just at the point where the stem is beginning to turn tough and woody. (Very young, tender asparagus won't need this treatment.)

Steam over boiling water in a steamer basket, or sauté in 2 tablespoons of butter over medium-high heat, for just a few minutes. Asparagus should be bright green and crisp-tender.

Top each serving with Toasted Tamari Almonds.

Toasted Tamari Almonds

1/2 **cup sliced almonds**
Tamari or shoyu
Butter or olive oil

Preheat the oven to 300°F.

Spread the sliced almonds in a shallow layer on a baking sheet and sprinkle with the tamari or shoyu and stir to moisten. Dot with butter or a little olive oil.

Bake the almonds, stirring often, for 10 minutes or so, keeping an eye on them (nuts burn easily). They will smell toasty and delicious when they're done, and they will have turned a rich and delicious golden brown. Make extra, if you like, so you can snack on these as you cook—they are highly addictive and delicious.

Risotto Primavera

serves 4

This delicious recipe is bursting with colors and springtime tastes. Think of Botticelli's famous painting *Primavera* as you chop and stir—both the painting and this sensually satisfying dish celebrate the pleasures of spring. It is important to use arborio rice, a special variety that produces risotto's luscious creaminess.

1 tablespoon olive oil
1 medium red onion, chopped
1 red bell pepper, seeded and diced
2 cups mushrooms, thickly sliced (you may use button mushrooms or a combination of varieties)
2 garlic cloves, minced
1½ cups arborio rice
4 cups vegetable stock or water
4 tablespoons chopped fresh parsley
½ teaspoon sea salt, or to taste
2 more cups vegetable stock or water
13 asparagus spears, washed and cut into 1-inch pieces (one spear for each moon of the year)
¼ cup grated Romano or Parmesan cheese (optional)

In a large saucepan, heat the olive oil. Add the red onion, pepper, mushrooms, and minced garlic. Cook, stirring frequently, for 8 minutes.

Stir in the rice, 2 cups of the vegetable stock or water, the parsley, and the sea salt. Bring to a simmer, then cook over low heat, uncovered, for about 10 minutes, stirring frequently.

Stir in the remaining 2 cups of vegetable stock or water and the asparagus. Continue to cook, stirring, until rice is tender, about 10 minutes.

Remove risotto from the heat and, if desired, fold in the grated cheese. Serve hot.

You could experiment with different vegetables for this dish: broccoli rabe, spinach, and garden peas could all be substituted for the asparagus.

Aphrodite's Love Cakes
makes about 1 dozen, depending on size

A lot of love-magic starts in the kitchen—sensual meals are often preludes to other sensual pleasures. Here, sweet little cakes blessed by the Greek goddess of love may inspire you to create some special tenderness in the bedroom. Share them with your partner or, if you are solo, have a few as a preface to some self-loving pleasure. Either way, these cakes will help to get you in the mood.

¼ cup whiskey or brandy

2 tablespoons dried damiana (a potent aphrodisiac herb; if your local natural foods store doesn't carry it, see Supplies)

2 tablespoons dried rose petals, crushed

½ cup whole wheat flour

½ cup unbleached white flour

½ cup rolled oats (oats are a great sexual tonic—the phrase "sow your wild oats" has a basis in fact)

2 teaspoons baking powder

½ teaspoon sea salt

½ teaspoon ground cinnamon

1 egg

½ cup honey (honey has long been sacred to the Goddess; here, it reminds us of the sweetness of love)

½ cup melted butter or oil

1 teaspoon vanilla extract

Dried coriander (traditional for both love and lust)

Preheat the oven to 350°F.

In a small bowl, place the whiskey or brandy, damiana, and rose petals. Steep this mixture for at least 15 minutes.

In a large mixing bowl, combine both flours, the oats, baking powder, sea salt, and ground cinnamon.

In a separate bowl, lightly beat the egg. Add the honey, oil or melted butter, and vanilla and stir to combine.

Add both bowls of wet ingredients to the dry ones in the large bowl and mix thoroughly.

Grease a baking sheet (you may want to draw magical—or erotic—patterns in the oil with your finger). Drop dough by tablespoonfuls onto the greased sheet, then sprinkle cakes with dried coriander. You may want to light a stick of sweet-smelling incense and blow a little smoke over the cakes before you pop them in the oven.

Bake for 10 to 12 minutes, or until lightly browned. Honey burns easily, so be careful not to overbake. Cakes will be soft, moist, and chewy.

everything blooms and ripens now—it is the time of
greatest light and warmth. To celebrate this exuberant season, call on these summer words:

summer's watchwords Abundant, fiery, fresh,
fruity, hot, juicy, rich, ripe, succulent, opulent

summer's scents and tastes Freshly cut cucumbers,
food cooking on a grill, watermelon, crushed mint,
the mouthwatering tang of lemons and limes, new-mown grass, fresh basil

part 5: s u m m e r

Setting the Stage for Summer

*T*he *perfect summer house* is ringed with shady trees and tangled flower beds. It is an easy dance from the garden to the kitchen—you saunter inside, hips swaying, your basket heavy with edible treasure. When you set the basket down, you stretch lazily, pausing for a moment to luxuriate in the vivid colors all around you, the sunshine blazing everywhere.

Wide French doors open out onto a terrace blooming with flowers and herbs in big terra-cotta pots. Scarlet tiles feel cool under your bare feet, and the wood-fired brick oven burns only in the early morning, before the day heats up, but its smoky scent follows you as you move from table to cupboard. You pause at the alcove in the wall, where a statue of the grain goddess sits smiling, a sheaf of wheat in her hand.

Beyond the windows, a landscape lush with green, fruits and vegetables shining like brightly colored jewels among the leaves. Indoors, bowls and baskets overflow with fresh foods—eggplants in their glossy purple glory, peppers in vivid hues of red and yellow and green, tomatoes sizzling with color and pungent scent, ears of corn with hair as silky and abundant as the Goddess's own. Melons, fruits, and berries, like little pregnant bellies, fill the kitchen with a fragrance sweet as honey, and your eyes close blissfully as the scent of fresh herbs wafts around you—dusty sage, shiny succulent basil, crisp thyme, pungent rosemary.

You can feel a passion for life lighting your body and spirit like a flame. As you begin preparing your evening meal—as you choose and chop and stir and taste—you realize that your act of cooking has become a joyous dance.

The Summer Kitchen

*L*uscious summer holds two special festivals in its warm arms: Litha, the great sun-fest of Summer Solstice in June, and the honoring of the bread, Lughnasad, on August 1. Decorating the summer kitchen, like celebrating these two special days, can be an exercise in having a little wild fun. Summer colors and shapes make us feel as vibrant and bountiful as this glorious season and can be used to encourage the growth and fulfillment of wishes, plans, or projects in many ways.

If you would like to feel more prosperous or fertile, you can align yourself with summer's energies by choosing to decorate your kitchen with green—leaf green, moss green, grass green—the color of growing things. Renew a tired kitchen chair with a coat of green paint, or find some old green tiles to make a backsplash for your sink. Paper leaves are fun to strew around the room in various ways, or you could paint leaves on any available surface, if you're artistically inclined. And green potted plants add their encouraging presence to your countertops or table.

For more confidence, warmth, or success, choose fiery red, sunny yellow, rich, buttery amber or goldenrod, mouthwatering tangerine. Sun colors have been associated for centuries with the oomph it takes to make things happen. Paint a big golden sun above your stove, or experiment with vivid rag rugs or hot-colored dinnerware.

And it's easy to make a connection with nature's abundant energy by picking a little wild beauty to honor in your kitchen—the earth is blooming in a thousand ways just outside your door. From the simple (a handful of dandelions or long grass plopped in a jar) to the more complex (fragrant blooms from the garden or a roadside patch of weeds, tendrils of berry-covered brambles, a bowl of ripe, dewy fruit), summer decorations are an evocation of bounty, richness, delight, and nourishment. By honoring the loveliness growing all around us, we invite summer's positive energies into our home.

As the season begins to wane after August 1, you may want to include the colors of wheat and golden corn in your decorations. Braided wheat figures or a wreath made of corn husks, or even a bunch of wheat-colored dried grasses for your table, all are beautiful ways to honor the Earth Mother's generosity to her children. See yourself as her representative. Every time you make a meal, you are echoing that goddesslike power to nourish both body and spirit.

Summer offers so many delights for the eye, the taste buds, and the soul! But most of us would rather dance and play outside rather than stir and chop and bake indoors for hours in the heat—and so the recipes here are simple and easy to prepare. Several dishes are meant to be cooked and eaten outdoors, surrounded by the chirping of insects and the trees' cooling green. Summer teaches us to relax and bask in the security of earth's bounty; what we need will be given to us. And summer's gifts are abundantly rich with flavor and color—every bite bursts in our mouths like fireworks that fill our bodies with vitality.

Summer Spell for a Sunny Will

Goodwill is certainly a concept to ponder. How many of us can truly say we have it? In summer, when warm colors and blazing vitality evoke the power of the will, we can align ourselves with our deepest, best selves with this simple, old spell.

You will need:

2 cups birdseed

Go to a place where wild birds are known to congregate (pigeons will do, for city-dwellers). Stand facing the sun. Close your eyes and imagine that the golden sunlight is streaming into your solar plexus, your will center. Now visualize that you are beaming that golden light back to the sun as you say:

My will be like the sun,
Golden light.
For the good of all,
Shine bright.

Now, carefully sprinkle the birdseed around yourself in as perfect a circle as you can, and say:

Lighten my will, to feed the world. Now it is done.

Step outside the circle and find a place to sit quietly and observe. Watch as the birds discover and feed themselves with your gift. As each bird takes flight after its meal, visualize your will center growing more light and generous and warm. Give some thought to the ways in which you can harness your immense fiery will in order to give something unique and meaningful to the world. When we do the things we most love to do, we nourish ourselves and others, for the good of all. Blessed be.

Early-Summer Recipes

Goddess's Green Pea Soup

serves 4 to 6

I discovered this unusual, delightful soup many, many Junes ago—it was the first consciously vegetarian recipe I ever made. The delicate flavor and beautiful green color are the very essence of early summer—and are such a lovely surprise. The nourishing ingredients are bursting with goodness straight from the Earth Mother. As you push those buttons on the blender, envision yourself as a Great Green Goddess, harnessing the power of the volt to turn little round green goodies into this glorious soup.

The fresher the peas you can find, the more vibrant your soup will be.

2 **cups hot water**
1 **cup cashews or** $^1/_3$ **cup cashew butter**
$^1/_4$ **cup onion, chopped**
1 **tablespoon olive oil**
1 **teaspoon sea salt**
1 **garlic clove**
1 **pound fresh (or frozen) tender green peas**
Sprigs of fresh mint, for garnish

In a blender or food processor, blend the water, cashews, chopped onion, olive oil, sea salt, and garlic until smooth.

Add the green peas and continue to blend until smooth.

Transfer to a saucepan. Thin to desired consistency with added hot water, and simmer over medium heat, stirring often, until soup is heated through. Serve immediately or chill for a minimum of 2 hours and serve cold. This soup is especially pleasing when served with a sprig of fresh mint in each bowl.

Flowering Salad

This lovely salad, like the flowering earth around us in early summer, delights the inner artist in all of us: Succulent greens starred with colorful blossoms make a feast for both eye and palate.

Use the freshest ingredients you can get your hands on. If you don't have a garden, explore your local farmer's market or produce stand—nothing beats the refreshing coolness of a just-picked cucumber, or the tenderness of young lettuce. Tart wood sorrel adds a delightful lemony note, and edible flowers nourish our spirit with their beauty.

1 **handful lettuce leaves per serving—choose from: mesclun, field greens, curly or red lettuces, spinach, or any combination of these**
Cucumber, peeled (unless organic) and cut into desired shapes
Sprigs of freshly picked wood sorrel (or 1 small tomato, cored and quartered)
A sprinkling of edible blossoms— choose from: nasturtium (peppery), borage (cucumber-like), calendula
Sea salt and freshly ground black pepper
Simple Summer Dressing (recipe follows)

For each serving, you'll need a few tender lettuce leaves. Experiment with unusual varieties—many supermarkets now carry organic lettuces and mixtures that are flavorful and rich in nutrients, as well as those that are more familiar. Arrange the greens artfully on a plate.

Next, cut the cucumber (peeled, if it's the waxed supermarket kind) into any shape you prefer: chunks, 1/4-inch rounds, half-moons, or long quarters.

Place the cucumber pieces on top of the bed of lettuce, along with several sprigs of wood sorrel. (This plentiful wild green is available in most yards at this time of year. Just be sure to avoid sprayed or contaminated areas. Look for sorrel's cloverlike leaves and tiny white or yellow flowers. If wood sorrel is unavailable, substitute a small, ripe tomato, cored and quartered.)

Decorate each salad with the flower heads. Dust the salad with sea salt and pepper to taste, and drizzle with Simple Summer Dressing, if desired.

Simple Summer Dressing   *serves 4*

¹/₃ cup extra-virgin olive oil
2 tablespoons red wine vinegar or
  freshly squeezed lemon juice
1 garlic clove, crushed

**Sea salt and freshly ground black
  pepper**

Combine the ingredients in a bowl and whisk until smooth.

Daylily-Bud Sauté

This scrumptious food was introduced to my family on a glorious Summer Solstice by Raven, weed-woman and friend. I had long been an admirer of beautiful daylily flowers, but I never knew you could eat them. What a concept! And such a simple dish—who ever said that recipes had to be complicated and time-consuming to be delicious? Daylily-Bud Sauté goes from gathering basket to table in minutes and is rich with the Earth Mother's wildness.

Daylilies are a glorious sign that summer has unfolded around us. Their brilliant orange trumpets, which bloom for only a single day before they curl and fade, remind us to truly enjoy our planet's gifts in the moment. We open our hands to the Earth Mother's bounty when we delight not only in the sight of the daylily's bright flower, but also in the taste and nourishment it offers.

Fresh daylily buds can usually be found in profusion all over—in your own yard or just around the corner. Pick only the firm unopened buds, and be sure that no sprays or chemicals were used wherever you find them.

1 **handful daylily buds per serving**
1 to 2 **tablespoons olive oil**
   Sea salt or tamari
1 **garlic clove, crushed (optional)**
1 **tablespoon chopped onion (optional)**

Gather a handful of buds for each serving you wish to make.

Sauté the buds over medium-high heat in 1 to 2 tablespoons of the olive oil. Season to taste with the sea salt or tamari. Throw in a clove of crushed garlic, if you wish, or a tablespoon or so of chopped onion for each serving. Enjoy every marvelous bite.

Juno's Summer Quiche

serves 4 to 6

This quiche celebrates the Roman goddess who also gave us the name for the month of June. Juno, once revered as an omnipotent goddess of female power, was gradually diminished by the patriarchy until she became merely the jealous, shrewish wife of the god Jupiter. But *we* know the real story! Her quiche is stuffed with fresh summer goodies that will help you to feel as strong and powerful as Juno in her prime. Tomatoes—both sundried and fresh—and sprigs of rosemary, added to the glories of fresh garden vegetables, give this quiche a Mediterranean flair that Juno doubtless would have enjoyed.

2 **tablespoons olive oil**
1 **medium onion, sliced thinly**
2 **garlic cloves, crushed**
2 **cups fresh spinach, coarsely chopped**
½ **cup julienned red bell pepper strips**
⅓ **cup oil-packed sundried**

   tomatoes, chopped
1 **9-inch Wholemeal Crust (recipe follows)**
2 **cups grated cheese (low-fat or nonfat, if you wish to reduce the fat in this dish)—choose from: Gruyère (the best), Jarlsberg, Swiss, Monterey Jack, Cheddar**

A combination of any of these:
>   3 tablespoons grated Parmesan or Romano cheese
>   1 tablespoon whole wheat flour
>   2 dashes of sea salt
> 2 to 3 eggs
> 1¹/₂ cups low-fat milk
>   1 medium tomato, thinly sliced
>   Fresh rosemary sprigs, for garnish
>   White pepper

Preheat the oven to 375°F.

In your favorite saucepan, heat the olive oil over medium-high. Add the onion and garlic, stirring frequently until vegetables are barely tender. Then add the spinach, pepper strips, and chopped sun-dried tomatoes. Continue cooking for several minutes.

Spread the vegetables evenly over an unbaked bottom crust in a 9-inch pie plate—use Wholemeal Crust or your favorite piecrust recipe. For an even more pronounced Roman flavor, you could make a simple polenta as the base for this quiche—try one of the excellent boxed mixes available nearly everywhere.

Sprinkle over the vegetables the grated cheese of your choice along with the grated Parmesan or Romano cheese, flour, and a dash of sea salt.

In a small bowl, whisk together the eggs, low-fat milk, and a dash of sea salt until smooth, and pour the resulting custard over the vegetables and cheese. Place tomato slices decoratively on top of the quiche, along with several fresh sprigs of rosemary. Grate some white pepper over all, in honor of Juno's notoriously peppery temper.

Pop the quiche in the oven and bake for 40 to 45 minutes, until puffy, fragrant, and golden brown. Then enjoy the beauty of your creation.

Wholemeal Crust

This delicate crust makes an excellent base for both quiches and sweet pies.

1/2 cup whole wheat or graham
    flour
1/2 cup unbleached white flour
Dash of sea salt
1/3 cup chilled butter, cut into
    small pieces
2 to 3 tablespoons ice water

Combine the whole wheat or graham flour, white flour, and a dash of sea salt in a bowl.

Using a pastry cutter or two knives, mix in the chilled butter. Continue to blend, rubbing the dough with your fingers if necessary, until the mixture resembles coarse meal.

Add 2 to 3 tablespoons of ice water and mix with your hands until the dough forms a ball.

Dust your surface with flour and roll out the dough until it is a flat circle 1 inch larger than your pie plate. Place it in the plate, pinching the edges decoratively if you wish. Then fill and bake as directed.

Simple Strawberry Shortcake   *serves 6*

Simple is good. At my favorite strawberry festival, held each year along the Hudson River in Beacon, New York, you can listen to some great old-fashioned folksinging while you stuff yourself with a quintessential, simple strawberry shortcake that absolutely melts in your mouth—my idea of the perfect summer experience.

Ideally, we should all be able to go out to our garden, or a pick-your-own farm down the road, and gather a basketful of fragrant strawberries, luscious with juice and flavor (the very thought makes my mouth water). But even the strawberries we buy at the grocery store are summer-wonderful, little evocations of the Goddess in all her scarlet glory. Either way, strawberries with whole wheat shortcake—a healthier and quicker version of the fat-laden classic requiring no rolling out (more time to play!)—are a healthy, delectable tribute to summer, wherever you live.

For the shortcake:
>   2 **cups whole wheat flour**
>   2 **tablespoons brown sugar**
>   1 **tablespoon baking powder**
>   1 **teaspoon baking soda**
> $^1/_2$ **teaspoon cinnamon**
> $^1/_4$ **teaspoon sea salt**
> $^1/_2$ **cup milk, buttermilk,**
>   **or soy milk**
>   2 **tablespoons vegetable oil**

For the filling and topping:
>   **Fresh strawberries, sliced**
>   **Whipped cream or yogurt**

Preheat the oven to 450°F.

In a mixing bowl, combine the whole wheat flour, brown sugar, baking powder, baking soda, cinnamon, and sea salt.

Stir into the flour mixture with a fork the vegetable oil and either milk, buttermilk, or soy milk, until moistened. Mixture will be sticky. Spread the dough in a lightly greased 8-inch square baking pan.

Bake for 10 to 15 minutes, until lightly browned. Cool for 5 minutes.

To serve, cut shortcake into six pieces. Split each piece and stuff with sliced fresh strawberries—and yogurt or whipped cream, if you like—then spoon more strawberries and whipped cream or yogurt on top. You have created a dessert fit for a goddess.

Litha Magic

Litha, the Summer Solstice, is the longest day of the year. When it arrives (between June 20 and 23), something of the intensity of this brief, peak moment enters into our hearts. We have only this one chance a year to celebrate the glorious, vibrant circle of the sun at its strongest and most powerful, and the energy we generate during this festival will remain as a warming reminder when the sun begins its inevitable decline toward autumn.

For centuries, especially in cold northern countries, the Solstice has been honored with a kind of fierce joy: After today, the days will grow shorter, but no matter how brutal the winter winds to come, this moment, this *now*, is warm and alive. And so we make crowns for ourselves from sunny daisies and other bright flowers, we hold hands and dance in a circle sunwise to honor the circuit of that great, fiery life-giver across the sky. And we give thought to the ways in which each of us shines for the world.

Kitchen Rituals for Litha

Try simply noticing the light outside your kitchen window, becoming aware of sun patterns on leaves and buildings, the colors of the shadows, the effortless way in which the sun can dry up a puddle or make a plant grow tall. Think about your own power to make things grow, to bring ideas and projects to fruition, to warm the people around you.

Choose golden, round things to eat today in honor of the sun, taking time to savor and appreciate the sunny shape and color and quality of the foods you fix. Something as simple as frying an egg or slicing an orange in rounds, if done with sun-consciousness, will make a satisfying connection with your inner Wild One and with the sun's vital power. If you feel like doing something more elaborate, you could make a round golden quiche (Juno's Summer Quiche is ideal), or stoke up the grill and cook with real, living flame. Summer Solstice is the perfect time to celebrate fire. And you could decorate your stove and oven—representatives of fire in your kitchen—with some sunny flowers.

Litha is a good day to put your handheld cooking utensils outside to soak up some sunshine and sun-energy. Then, whenever you use them in the dark and chilly winter to come, you will remember this simple, powerful act and be heartened.

Decorate your table with daisies, noticing how the rays of petals surrounding their golden centers mimic the round fiery life-giver in the sky. Breathe your wishes for the harvest to come into the flowers, and know that your own precious life-energy will help to create whatever you want and need.

Spell for Removing Barriers to Success

There is absolutely no reason that we cannot all be deeply successful, creating lives rich with meaning and purpose that feed us, body and soul, for the good of all. Working with the abundant sun-energy of Litha gives us an added boost in that direction.

You will need:

> **A magnifying glass**
> **A piece of paper**
> **A pencil or pen**

First, give yourself time and space to go deep. Begin to turn your thoughts toward all the things your inner troll voices have been telling you, the things that keep you from being successful in the deepest and most meaningful sense. Write them all down on your paper—"I'm not good enough, I don't have enough talent, I don't deserve success"—whatever they are.

Crumple up the paper into a ball. Go outside and find a safe surface that will contain fire without damage: a sidewalk, a barbecue grill, a bare spot in your yard. Holding the crumpled paper, ask the midsummer sun for help in removing these obstacles to your success. With the magnifying glass, focus the sun on the ball of paper in as tight a spot as you can. It may take a little practice before you get it just right, but when you do, something miraculous will happen: The bright spot will smoke and then flare into flame. Soon your barriers will be reduced to ash. Give thanks to the sun and let the wind carry the ashes away. Now take a moment to let the sun charge you with good intentions and good energy. When we allow ourselves to shine, we encourage everyone in our orbit to shine as well.

Inner Fire Meditation

You will need:

> **1 big yellow onion**
> **1 tablespoon olive oil**
> **Cayenne pepper**
> **1 slice fresh bread**

Set your onion in the sun for an hour or so and then pick it up in your hand. Feel its warmth. Stroke its breastlike shape. Close your eyes and take a long, lingering sniff.

Now slowly peel off the outer skin. Really notice the papery dryness as it is sloughed off, and the dewy freshness of the layers beneath. Hold the onion to your lips and savor its warm, smooth kiss. Now find your trusty wooden chopping board and a good knife. Chop your onion slowly and carefully. Notice how your knife invokes the juice. Can you stand the onion's sudden pungency? Are your eyes streaming?

Heat a saucepan and 1 tablespoon of olive oil and add your chopped onion. Sauté it slowly, enjoying the roundness of the pan, like a little hot sun in your kitchen, magically changing your onion from hard, white, and opaque, to soft, golden, and translucent. Add some cayenne (as much as you can stand!), and watch the colors changing as you stir. Your pan is sizzling now with sun-energy.

Toast a slice of good fresh bread and spread it with your sautéed onions and cayenne. As you savor the strong, hot flavors, think about your inner fire. We have sun-power inside us, too—power to make things change. Fire makes us feel zesty and energized. A mouthful of cayenne can make the stodgiest of us yelp and run for water. A spirit full of fire can change the stuff around us that needs changing. How will you use your fire? What are the fruits of your life right now? What are you creating? Whether it is a peaceful, loving home, or a garden, or a quiet spot in the shade for loved ones to rest and feel recharged; whether it is a book, a play, a symphony, or a painting that wraps an entire wall in movement and color; whether you are creating a community, a special friendship, an altar under the trees, or a loaf of good bread—the warm power of the sun in summer invites you to create, to produce, to make it happen.

Hot Summer Peach Play for Lovers

This summer frolic is messy beyond belief, but it's also a wonderful way to celebrate the sensuality of summer and the joy of the Solstice with a loving partner.

Find the ripest, sweetest, juiciest peach you can. First, take turns holding it, sniffing it, stroking its fuzziness, touching it gently to your lips, to your cheek, then letting your tongues explore its skin. Gently break it in two. Taste its juice.

Now, softly and slowly, caress each other with the open peach—remove the pit, and then stroke its flesh all over each other. Gradually increase the pressure until you have globs of peach oozing delightfully everywhere. Then, savoring the experience, lick each other until all traces of peach are gone. (Well, *almost* all traces: This activity will probably get pretty sticky.) If you are performing this exercise outdoors, be prepared for buggy visitors who will be irresistibly drawn to your warm stickiness. Making love covered with peach goop is a unique summer experience. And when it all gets to be a bit much, you can race each other for the shower or go jump in a lake—then afterglow turns into a refreshing tingle.

Song of the Litha Goddess

She weaves the world into grasses and fruit,

She winds the world in her hair.

Ablaze with radiant power her face glows, clear light of the sun.

Blessings of golden fire upon you, of round sweet days

Circling each other like wheels,

And of the bounty, the beauty of ripe, fertile earth.

My starry blessings, my sunny blessings upon you—

Shine now and always in your hearts.

Midsummer Recipes

 ## Titania's Cherry Soup

This midsummer night's dream of a first course would be right at home in a fairy court, sipped under the trees from tiny acorn cups. Its ambrosial flavor and delicate pink color make it a favorite with children, too. Titania's Cherry Soup reminds us of the summer orchards that rain delicious fruits down upon our heads with such amazing generosity.

$2^1/_2$ **pounds fresh, dark sweet cherries**
  4 **cups water**
 $^1/_4$ **cup (or more to taste) honey,
    brown rice syrup, or maple syrup**
Juice of 1 lemon
**Whipped cream or yogurt as topping
   (optional)**

Wash and pit the cherries and place in a saucepan with the water and honey, brown rice syrup, or maple syrup. Bring to a boil, then reduce heat and simmer for 15 to 20 minutes.

Remove 24 cherries and reserve.

Blend the remaining cherries and liquid with the lemon juice, and additional honey or syrup, if needed (taste and see), until smooth.

Chill thoroughly.

To serve, ladle the soup into your prettiest bowls and top with the reserved cherries and a dollop of yogurt or whipped cream, if desired.

Midsummer Salad

A round salad bowl filled with crisp, juicy, brightly colored vegetables makes a sunny centerpiece for your midsummer table.

Part of the fun of preparing this dish is using only what you like, only the freshest vegetables available. Taste the pleasures of exploration as you open a dark red beet—there are circles inside! Relish the vivid stripes of sliced red cabbage, or the blazing colors of peppers—experiment with yellow, orange, and purple ones, or fresh chilies with their varying shades of pale yellow-green.

Midsummer Salad is all about making tasty, vivid choices. Enjoy the many variations you can create to please yourself and your loved ones. The spicy heat and colorful beauty of the results will echo the summer world outside your doors.

A colorful selection of vegetables— choose from:

Hot-colored bell peppers, julienned (try yellow, orange, and red)

Beets, cut into thin circles or small cubes

Red onion, thinly sliced or chopped

Red cabbage, chopped

Fresh jalapeño peppers or other hot peppers, thinly sliced or chopped

Tomatoes, quartered, sliced, or chopped (experiment with unusual varieties—yellow or orange tomatoes add interest and excitement to your bowl)

Red radishes, sliced

Carrots, thinly sliced or julienned

Fresh basil, parsley, or cilantro, chopped

Juice of half a lemon (optional)

In a large salad bowl, combine any or all of the vegetables.

Toss the salad with the juice of half a lemon, or with your favorite dressing, and serve.

Smoky Summer Vegetables on the Grill (or under the Broiler)

There is something truly magical about grilling. Our ancestors knew the mystery of sitting all together around flames that turned to glowing coals that—miraculously—transformed raw foods and gave them a special, smoky flavor touched by fire. Deep inside ourselves, we remember.

This simple recipe uses the power of fire in a way that our ancestors would have understood and enjoyed. The grill (or fire pit or broiler) becomes a small emblem of the transformative sun that is making its power felt in so many positive ways at this time of year. Vegetables off the grill have a mouthwatering pungency that makes them both unusual and delicious. Don't be surprised if your vegetable-hating youngsters ask for seconds.

Part of the pleasure of this recipe lies in choosing the perfect vegetables to honor in the flames. When we really linger over the textures, colors, and shapes of eggplant, squash, or peppers, we allow our senses to be entranced. (See Things to Do with Grilled Vegetables on page 186 for suggestions on ways to enjoy leftover vegetables from your feast.)

Fresh vegetables—choose from:
  Whole ears of corn, husked and cleaned
  Green or red bell peppers, cut lengthwise into 1-inch strips
  Zucchini or yellow summer squash, cut lengthwise in quarters
  Red or white onions, cut into wedges
  Portabella or other mushrooms, sliced thickly
  Small to medium-sized eggplants, cut in 1/2-inch rounds
  Olive oil or a Midsummer Marinade (recipes follow)

Brush any or all of the suggested vegetables with good-quality olive oil (or marinate in any of the following Midsummer Marinades), and then arrange them evenly on a hot grill or underneath a hot broiler. Keep an eye on the vegetables and turn them as necessary—when they are flecked with char and are crisp-tender, they're done. Remove the vegetables to a serving platter as they reach the perfect doneness. Eggplant and onion usually take the longest to cook.

Midsummer Marinades

The basic ingredient for these recipes is olive oil, with varied additions to produce different flavorful delights.

In every case, whisk the ingredients together and allow vegetables to soak in the resulting marinade for at least 30 minutes before grilling. Each recipe may be doubled or tripled as needed.

Hot Mama Marinade
- $^1/_3$ cup tamari or shoyu
- $^1/_4$ cup olive oil
- 1 teaspoon dried mustard
- $^1/_2$ to 1 teaspoon cayenne pepper (or more, depending on how hot you like it)
- 1 tablespoon Tabasco sauce (optional)
- 2 or 3 garlic cloves, crushed

Sweet and Tangy Marinade
- $^1/_3$ cup tamari or shoyu
- $^1/_4$ cup olive oil
- $^1/_4$ cup maple syrup or honey
- Juice of 1 lemon

Herbed Red Wine Marinade
- $^1/_2$ cup full-bodied red wine
- $^1/_4$ cup olive oil
- 2 garlic cloves, crushed
- 1 teaspoon sea salt
- $^1/_2$ teaspoon each of any of the following dried herbs (or 1 teaspoon each, if fresh; or place whole sprigs of fresh herbs on vegetables as they grill)—choose from: rosemary, marjoram, thyme, oregano, basil, sage, or any combination of these

Things to Do with Grilled Vegetables

Leftover grilled vegetables can become the basis of many nourishing and delicious summer meals, with minimal effort on your part.

- Try them plain on whole grain bread. Stuff a baguette with them. Add a slice of provolone or some grated mozzarella—or Gruyère—and melt under the broiler. Or make special garlic bread by adding the grilled veggies, chopped fine, to the crushed garlic cloves.

- Make a rich and flavorful pasta sauce by simply mixing them with your favorite cooked pasta. You could also add a tomato, peeled and chopped, and a crushed garlic clove.

- Add to pasta salads or your regular tossed garden salads.

- Chop fine; add a can of garbanzo beans, drained and mashed, and a clove of crushed garlic. Use as a dip for pita or flatbread. Or add salsa and scoop it up with a taco chip. Chopped grilled vegetables are also delicious wrapped in large basil leaves.

- Grilled vegetables go well with rice, pilafs, couscous, and bulghur.

- Make your own mouthwatering burritos by filling flour tortillas with grilled vegetables, mashed cooked beans, salsa, and cheese.

- Add to your favorite gazpacho recipe. Or simply whiz the vegetables in a blender, thinning to the desired consistency with lemon juice and vegetable broth for a delicious chilled soup. Top with a dollop of sour cream, if desired.

Fiery Red Beans and Rice

serves 6

At the hottest time of the year, our thoughts inevitably turn to cultures that thrive on heat, and whose cuisines reflect a passion for spice. Rice and beans are a staple food for many people. This version—rich with tender vegetables and redolent with flavor—uses chipotle pepper to give it a special smoky taste. Fiery Red Beans and Rice becomes a delicious celebration of summer heat. Make it in honor of Akewa, the Argentine sun goddess who tells us that we are her sisters—only we are stranded here on earth while she remains in the sky.

2 to 3 tablespoons olive oil
1 medium onion, chopped
2 to 3 garlic cloves, crushed
1 medium green bell pepper, seeded and chopped
1 medium dried chipotle pepper, coarsely chopped
1 teaspoon dried oregano
$1/2$ teaspoon cumin
$1/2$ teaspoon sea salt
$1/2$ teaspoon cayenne pepper (more or less, to taste)
1 cup long-grain rice
$2^1/2$ cups vegetable broth or water
1 15-ounce can small red beans, drained
3 tablespoons chopped fresh parsley

In a large saucepan, heat the olive oil over medium-high heat until fragrant. Then add the onion, garlic, green pepper, chipotle pepper, oregano, cumin, and the sea salt and cayenne to taste. Cook the vegetables, stirring often, for 10 to 15 minutes, until very tender.

Add the rice, stirring to coat with the oil. Then add the vegetable broth or water and red beans and bring to a boil. Cover, then simmer for 25 minutes, until rice is tender. Stir in the parsley and serve.

Enchanted Berries

This dish is sheer elfin enchantment when served after dark on a midsummer's night: The flickering of its mysterious violet-blue flames remind us of magical winged creatures glimmering in the shadows just beyond our reach.

If you have wild black or red raspberries in your own backyard or a mulberry tree that wants to share its sweet, subtle fruit, enlist the aid of friends and loved ones and pick a basketful—berries we've picked ourselves taste better than any other kind. But Enchanted Berries is also a magical way to enjoy the abundance of fresh raspberries you can find at any market this time of year.

Keep in mind that the alcohol in this recipe burns off, so children can feast upon it without a qualm on your part.

3 **cups wild berries or fresh raspberries, at room temperature or even warmer**
1 **tablespoon brown sugar**
1/4 **cup brandy, cognac, or dark rum, at room temperature or warmer**
 Yogurt or whipped cream as topping (optional)

Place the wild berries or fresh raspberries into a flameproof chafing dish or bowl and sprinkle them with the brown sugar.

Pour the alcohol over the berries. Cover the dish or bowl for a moment, then uncover and light the berries carefully with a match.

Watch the magic flames breathlessly until they're gone, then serve the berries with a dollop of yogurt or whipped cream, if desired.

Lughnasad Magic

*F*or many *western Europeans*—even in Christian times—August 1 was a traditional holy day in honor of the first grain harvest, called Lammas (literally, "loaf-mass"). But Lughnasad has its origins in legend as a festival devised by Lugh, a Celtic sun god, in honor of the hardworking agricultural goddess Tailtiu, his foster mother. It is the quintessential festival day for this book, since it celebrates the sacredness of food, the body of Mother Earth, in the form of bread. The day offers us a chance to connect deeply with a central mystery: the fact that we both shape and are shaped by our lives, that we are, magically, both baker and bread.

Bread as sacrament is certainly no stranger to the Judeo-Christian culture. But for witches everywhere, Lughnasad is a celebration of the sacredness of *all* bodies and *all* food. On this day, my community spends several sunny hours forming dough into tiny individual shapes, each as different and unique as its maker. While the breads bake, we tell stories or make art together—one year,

 a local weaver inspired us to create a community weaving, everyone adding bits of grass, ribbon, and yarn to the web stretched between two trees. After the breads are baked, we carry them in grand procession to the center of our labyrinth, where each celebrant journeys to be fed, and to feed others. The ritual often ends at dusk by torchlight. With the taste of fresh bread in our mouths, and a feeling of deep nourishment in our hearts, we give our thanks to the planet that sustains us.

Kitchen Rituals for Lughnasad

Most of us simply don't have the time to bake regularly the way our great-grandmothers and great-great-grandmothers did. But if you do just a little planning in advance, most of us can usually carve out the time to bake bread once a year, beginning on this day. By slowing down and savoring each step of the process, we rediscover the blessings of bread with our hands, our hearts, and our starved spirits.

When your loaves are done, you may want to bless them by singing a song over them, or saying a prayer, or wafting a smudge stick or incense wand over them—or by simply touching them with your hands. Now tear off a piece of your bread and place it in your mouth. Close your eyes as you taste it. It is amazing how different we feel about food when we cook it with the conscious intention of honoring its sacredness.

You can save a tiny bit of your special, sacred bread to place at your kitchen altar. Or wrap a piece in cloth and tuck it away until next year, when you can burn it outdoors or compost it, giving it back to the earth with thanks before you taste the first piece of your new bread. When we actively participate in simple, cyclical rituals like this one, year after year, we feel a sense of connection that goes a long way toward healing our spirit-wounds.

You may also want to make or buy a small wheat figure (or corn dolly) today. These harvest blessings were traditional in many cultures to honor the spirit of the wheat and bring luck and protection to the home. Craft shops also sell lovely sheaves of wheat or barley, which are easy to soak and braid. Tie your braid with a green ribbon and hang it over your oven. Or gather some dried grasses and do the same.

Spell to Bless Your Oven

The oven is an ancient emblem of transformation. Raw bread dough is one thing, but baked bread is clearly another; what comes out of the oven is quite different from what went in. We can honor the oven and its almost alchemical magic—its ability to change things in order to nourish us more deeply—with this simple spell.

You will need:

A cookie sheet
Flour

On the cookie sheet, which represents the earth, sprinkle a tiny amount of flour. Flour combines all four elements—it was rooted in earth, nourished by rain, warmed by sun, and harvested from air. Give some thought to this as you use your index finger to draw a simple sun-shape on the flour. The oven is like the sun, a small, personal source of fire and heat. Breathe your own energy over the cookie sheet and then say the following:

A blessing on food and fed,
Earth and sun. All are one.
A blessing on your power.
Bless fire and food and maker
Bless seed and plant and baker.
Nourish us deeply,
Change us completely,
Teach us to nourish each other.

Shaping-Our-Lives Meditation

Bread baking is, in itself, a meditation. You could make one of the special bread recipes below to celebrate the transformative power of this festival day. Or you could try the following, which honors the ways in which we ourselves are the bread, kneaded, shaped, and baked by our lives.

 Sit in the sun, if possible, with a lump of dough or clay (one of the commercial modeling compounds will do in a pinch; or you could get some directly from the earth, if you know of a clay bed nearby; or buy air-dry clay at the local arts and crafts store; or make a salt, flour, and water dough; or use an extra bit of bread dough). Close your eyes, and, as you begin to warm the dough in your hands, give some thought to the ways in which we are all formed and shaped by the circumstances of our lives: the events that happen to us as children, the choices we make as adults, our genetic heritage, all the accidents, the patterns of personal destiny, the conscious and unconscious forces that pummel and knead us into our present shape. What are some of these for you?

With your eyes still closed, begin to shape the dough, simply allowing your hands and arms to move with it in ways that feel satisfying and good to you. When you have reached a place that feels complete, open your eyes and regard what you have made, with openness and no judgment. What does it look like? Remind you of?

The fire of difficulty takes our raw dough and bakes it, so that we become more nourishing human beings—or it hardens our clay so we can serve as strong vessels for the things life wishes us to hold. What have been some of the difficult circumstances that have baked you? Place your shaped dough in the sun, allowing that primal fire to dry and harden it. Before sunset, bring the dough indoors and keep it where you can be reminded of your own shaping and baking process.

Special Festival Recipes

These two breads celebrate the gifts of grain and harvest. They also give us the blessing of *slowing down*. All of nature begins to slow down at Lughnasad. We can too. We live such stressful lives; studies prove the correlation between stress and depression,

now epidemic in our crazy, driven culture. Let's celebrate our ability to take time, to live in a way that is gentler to ourselves and to our planet.

Real Earth-Mother Whole Grain Bread   *makes two loaves*

Don't be daunted by the thought of making your own bread. It's really not difficult, and the time it takes is filled with pleasures, not just a chore to be suffered through. You actually spend more time waiting than anything else: waiting for the yeast to bubble, waiting for the stuff to cool, waiting for the dough to rise, waiting for it to rise again. This gives you lots of time to relax and dream. In fact, bread-baking is great for reducing stress. And the fragrance of baking bread is definitely aromatherapeutic.

½ **cup warm water (105°F to 115°F)**
2 **tablespoons active dry yeast**
1½ **cups milk**
2 **cups rolled oats**
3 **tablespoons honey**
2 **tablespoons vegetable oil**
1 **teaspoon sea salt**
½ **cup sesame seeds (optional)**
4 **cups whole wheat flour**

First, you have to wake up your yeast. Place the warm water in a small bowl, and sprinkle the yeast over it. Let this stand in a warm spot until the yeast bubbles, about 5 minutes.

Scald the milk, then put it in a large mixing bowl and stir in the rolled oats.

Add the honey, vegetable oil, sea salt, and sesame seeds (if desired).

Cool mixture to lukewarm and add 2 cups of the whole wheat flour. Beat well with a wooden spoon. Then add the yeast mixture and beat some more.

Add the remaining 2 cups of whole wheat flour to make a soft dough. Turn out onto a floured surface and knead gently until smooth and elastic, about 10 minutes. (This is the really fun part. Kneading good dough is a sensual experience—it's warm, yielding, fleshy. Mmmm!)

Place the dough in a lightly oiled bowl, turning it so that all of its surface is

 oiled. Cover with a clean dish-towel and let it rise in a warm place until doubled in size, about 1 hour.

Punch down the dough. Divide it in half and let it rest 10 minutes. Shape into two round loaves and place on a lightly greased baking sheet. Cover and let rise until doubled, about 40 minutes.

Toward the end of that 40 minutes, preheat the oven to 350°F. Bake your loaves for 30 to 35 minutes, until golden brown. (Just wait until your home fills with bread-baking fragrance—an earthly paradise!) When the bread is done, the bottom crust will sound hollow when tapped. Take your loaves off the baking sheet immediately and let them cool on a rack.

You did it! Enjoy.

Shuck Bread

makes about 10 small breads

This recipe is a lot of fun to make, looks charming when done, and is deliciously satisfying. It makes a good alternative for people with sensitivities to wheat, or for those of you who prefer to honor the traditional bread festival by spending a few hours relaxing outdoors near a campfire rather than making bread in the kitchen. (In fact, this is a variation of a Girl Scout recipe given to me by Jessica Kemper, dear sister and superwoman, who has made this bread on camping trips with the troop.) And Shuck Bread teaches us to use every bit of the corn, shucks as well as kernels. (After you've finished scraping the cobs, you could carve them into little goddesses and leave them to dry in the sun. Then you can place one on your kitchen windowsill as a perpetual reminder of this warm and glorious festival day.)

1 cup fine-ground yellow cornmeal
⅓ cup fresh corn, scraped right off the cob (reserve leftover husks)
1 egg
2 tablespoons melted butter or mild-tasting olive oil

1 teaspoon baking powder
½ teaspoon sea salt
Water (enough to form a thick dough)
¾ cup shredded cheese (optional)

¼ **cup chopped jalapeño peppers (optional)**
Oil for coating husks
Sea salt and butter as seasoning (optional)

In a large bowl, combine the cornmeal, corn, egg, olive oil or melted butter, baking powder, sea salt, and water (as needed)—along with the shredded cheese and jalapeño peppers (if desired)—until the mixture forms a thick dough.

Choose two or three thicknesses of husks from your fresh corn for each Shuck Bread. Stack the husks together, insides facing up, and lightly brush the top husk with oil. Place 2 to 3 tablespoons of dough mixture in the center of this bed of husks.

Fold the husk edges so that the dough is completely encased in a long corn-shaped package. Tie each end shut, using a long strip of husk or string.

Wrap each bread with aluminum foil and place the little packages in the coals of a campfire or grill. (If you don't have a campfire handy, you may boil or steam these, or panfry them in a little vegetable oil, or bake them at 400°F.)

Bake until bread resists light finger pressure (it will stop feeling pasty). Untie one end of each package and fold shucks down—it will look charmingly like an ear of corn. Sprinkle with sea salt and butter, if you like, and eat.

Song of the Lughnasad Goddess

Mellow, homey, and brown, up to her elbows in flour,

She wipes her forehead and smiles.

She breaks off a piece of warm bread, sweet as honey,

Holds it up to your lips, then places her hand on your heart.

I am the ground beneath your feet,

The loving support for all your doing,

Sweetness of food and of feeding.

I am the hands that shape you.

I teach you strong lessons,

The wisdom of learning in fire.

Late-Summer Recipes

Tomato Venus Soup

serves 4 to 6

Did you know that tomatoes were once known as love apples and are sacred to Venus? And did you know that Venus is not only the ancient Roman goddess of love—but she's also the goddess of kitchen gardens? This Venusian treat is one of my favorite summer soups—effortless to make, but with a surprisingly complex taste that evokes warm days and sun-drenched earth. Its vivid color and mouthwatering flavor are sure to please. Make a potful tonight for the ones you love.

1 quart canned crushed tomato
3 to 4 ripe, large tomatoes, chopped
1/4 cup oil-packed sundried tomatoes, drained and chopped
1/4 cup red onion, chopped fine
1 garlic clove, crushed
2 tablespoons chopped fresh basil, or 1 tablespoon dried
2 tablespoons olive oil
2 tablespoons freshly squeezed lemon juice
Sea salt or tamari
Freshly ground black pepper
1 or 2 tablespoons melted butter (optional)

Sour cream as topping (optional)
4 to 6 fresh basil leaves, for garnish

In a bowl, if serving chilled, or in a saucepan, if you plan to serve warm, combine the crushed tomatoes, chopped tomatoes, and sundried tomatoes, red onion, garlic, basil, olive oil, lemon juice, and sea salt (or tamari) and black pepper to taste.

If you're serving this soup warm, you may want to add 1 or 2 tablespoons of melted butter. Warm or cold, it's delicious with a dollop of sour cream and a small fresh basil leaf for each serving.

Crunchy Summer Salads

Late summer is seed time, when the Earth Mother sends her energies into those little packages of power that will rest in the winter's earth and then waken to make new life in spring. We can enjoy the tasty nutrients that are so concentrated in seeds—and make our tossed salads late-summer special—by adding any of the following seeds to our garden greens.

pumpkin seeds, raw or toasted with tamari and cayenne • shelled sunflower seeds • sesame seeds• poppy seeds • dock seeds

Dock seeds add crunch and a pleasing reddish brown color—and you may find them in your own backyard. You could even try adding a few seeds from your bell peppers, rather than tossing them in the compost!

Simple-Gifts Millet

serves 4 to 6

Millet, which many of us used to think was for the birds, is now being rediscovered as a delicious and economical source of excellent nutrition—certainly not just so much birdseed.

Millet is one of nature's simplest but most delightful gifts; it is the perfect summer offering because its adorably round and golden grains are so reminiscent of the summer sun. Its delicate, nutlike taste makes a perfect foil for Mama Zabetta's Spicy Stir-Fried Greens (recipe follows).

1 **cup millet**
2 **cups water**
$^{1}/_{2}$ **teaspoon sea salt, or less to taste**
1 **garlic clove, crushed (optional)**
1 **tablespoon butter (optional)**
Toasted sesame seeds (optional)

Rinse the millet in warm water several times to remove any bitterness, then drain. Place in a saucepan with the water and add sea salt to taste.

Bring to a boil, cover, reduce heat to low, and simmer for 30 to 40 minutes, until water is completely absorbed.

For a variation on this recipe add a crushed garlic clove to the cooking millet, or 1 tablespoon of butter, or some toasted sesame seeds. Or you could cook your millet in vegetable broth rather than water.

Serve cooked millet plain, with butter if desired, or topped with Mama Zabetta's Spicy Stir-Fried Greens. Leftover cooked millet may be tossed with chopped vegetables and a simple salad dressing for a quick and delicious cold salad.

Mama Zabetta's Spicy Stir-Fried Greens with Nuts and Seeds
serves 4 to 6

Mama Zabetta (a.k.a. Elizabeth Cunningham—novelist, dear friend, and fellow food-lover) cooked this up for us one steamy late-summer evening and the resulting feast became a true celebration of the season, enjoyed with gusto by all. Redolent with tastes and textures, this spicy dish reminds us of both heat and bounty—two of summer's favorite watchwords.

Half the fun of preparing this luscious dish is adding things with a playful, liberal hand. As Zabetta forcefully reminds us, "Less isn't more. MORE is more!" Cast the crushed red pepper flakes about the pan with goddesslike generosity.

Be sure to keep adding olive oil whenever needed—the result should be moist and humid, never dry. Greens should predominate in this dish, but the choice of ingredients and their amounts is strictly up to you. Embrace your witchy power!

2 to 3   tablespoons olive oil
    Onions, chopped
    Garlic cloves, chopped
    Dried mustard
    Chilies or pepper flakes

Assorted slower-cooking
    vegetables—choose from:
    beets, bell peppers, zucchini
    or summer squash,
    cauliflower, and broccoli

Tamari or shoyu
Dry red wine (optional)
Assorted faster-cooking
    vegetables—choose from:
    Swiss chard, beet greens, and
    chinese cabbage
Toasted sesame seeds or sunflower
    seeds
Cashew, pecan, or almond pieces
Toasted sesame oil
Fresh parsley, chopped

Heat olive oil in a large saucepan or wok over medium-high heat until fragrant. Add the onions, garlic, dried mustard, and chilies or pepper flakes. Stir occasionally until vegetables are golden and tender.

Meanwhile, chop any or all of the slower-cooking vegetables and add, along with a sprinkle of tamari or shoyu and dry red wine, if desired.

Add olive oil as needed to keep ingredients shiny and moist. Stir occasionally, preferably while swigging an icy-cold beer. Add some more red pepper flakes or chilies. And maybe a little more tamari.

When everything is just crisp-tender, chop any or all of the faster-cooking vegetables and add, continuing to cook for just a couple of minutes, until the greens are barely wilted.

Add a handful or so of toasted sesame seeds or sunflower seeds and either cashew, pecan, or almond pieces.

Drizzle with toasted sesame oil and toss. Serve topped with chopped fresh parsley over a bed of your favorite cooked grain—brown rice, bulghur, couscous, quinoa, or Simple-Gifts Millet.

Sunny Peach Pie

serves 8

The amber glory of this sun-shaped dessert, as well as its mouthwatering aroma and flavor, satisfies us deeply in many ways. When we create a little sun that feeds us so deliciously, our hearts are warmed by this embodiment of the sun's power. Celebrate that power in yourself. And if you are so inclined, you could try making your sun-connection even stronger by baking this pie in the early morning as you watch the sun come up. As you arrange your peach slices in their circular pattern, think of the Scandinavian goddess Sunna, who sits and spins with her golden distaff so that the sun will rise.

1 unbaked pie crust—try Classic No-Dairy Crust (page 77), Wholemeal Crust (page 173), or Graham Cracker Crust (recipe follows)
3 to 4 cups sliced fresh peaches
2 teaspoons unbleached flour
¼ cup peach preserves (the kind with no added sugar)
1 teaspoon freshly squeezed lemon juice
½ teaspoon ground cinnamon
Freshly grated nutmeg
Dash of sea salt

Preheat the oven to 400°F.

In the unbaked crust of your choice, arrange the peach slices, in overlapping concentric circles. Sprinkle the peaches with the flour.

Combine the peach preserves, lemon juice, cinnamon, nutmeg, and a dash of sea salt in a saucepan and heat until hot while stirring.

Pour this glaze over the peaches and bake for 10 minutes, then turn the heat down to 375°F and continue baking for an additional 30 to 35 minutes. May be served warm, at room temperature, or cold.

Graham Cracker Crust

This simple recipe makes a tasty base for baked fruit pies.

³/₄ cup crushed graham crackers
¹/₄ cup melted butter

In a medium bowl, thoroughly combine the crushed graham crackers and melted butter.

Press firmly into the bottom of a 9-inch pie plate.

Fill and bake as directed in fruit-pie recipes.

Witchy Tips for Acting Out in the Kitchen

*T*he kitchen is the perfect place to honor our feelings. Many of us spend a lot of time there, often alone. We have a Power Place in the kitchen that feels like a safe space. What better spot to act out our aggressions and frustrations (as well as our more positive emotions) than in the kitchen?

Action and intention can be powerful allies when we cook. When we give our inner Wild Woman a conscious activity to perform, one that is rooted in what we are feeling right now, we place our feet on the path toward greater self-acceptance. Most of us are busy trying to heal ourselves from the deadly effects of our culture; our time in the kitchen can be used wisely and well to nurture that process along.

Here are a few ideas to help you get started. You will doubtlessly find your own ways to practice self-healing in the kitchen.

For those emotional, weepy days: Chop a lot of onions. Let the tears flow. Make exaggerated crying noises.

For excess anger and aggression: Try the karate method of peeling garlic cloves. Place the clove on a chopping board. With a hefty kitchen knife in your hand, focus your anger on the clove (it won't mind), take a deep breath, place the handle flat on the garlic, and whap it hard with your fist, yelling, *"Hi-yah!"* if desired. For serious anger, buy plates for a nickel at the thrift shop and throw them in the sink. The sound of breaking crockery is very releasing.

When you're in the process of shedding old, outgrown stuff in your life: Peel some root vegetables with a peeler (this is a good idea if your produce is not organic). As the curls of skin come peeling off, enjoy the freshness of the surface underneath. Imagine your own life beginning fresh and new.

To get your energies going: Shake up a batch of salad dressing in a jar. Get your whole body into the act. Be rhythmic. Let your jar of dressing become your maracas. Sing a Latino song. Shake those hips.

When you're feeling peaceful and calm (or to get yourself that way): Cook something that takes a lot of slow stirring (like Risotto Primavera, for instance). Let yourself drift and dream as you stir. Stirring can help us feel more sensuous, too.

When you feel confused or spacey: After you chop something into a pile, push it around on your chopping board and make patterns with it. Order your ingredients according to color. Clean out a drawer or cupboard.

When you're afraid: Sit on the countertop with your feet in the sink and run warm water on them. Hold something in your hand that grew in the ground—a potato, a beet, a turnip. Remind yourself that you are a child of the Earth Mother.

When you need to synthesize or get something together: Blending is great for this. It is pure magic to see how several very disparate things will homogenize beautifully after just a few seconds in the blender. Use a pureed soup recipe—Goddess's Green Pea or Sensuous Spinach, for instance.

When you want to feel more in touch with nature: Try a wild foods recipe, like Wild Salad, White Pine Tea, or Daylily-Bud Sauté. Going outside and gathering the ingredients is guaranteed to lift your spirits and make you feel more connected to the Earth Mother.

When you can't stand the thought of cooking: Take a trip to a farmer's market or natural foods store. Look for ingredients so fresh that they practically vibrate with energy, or for other more unusual things that will interest you.

Reading fiction is another way to get motivated in the kitchen. Years ago, a book-loving friend confided, "I always crave the foods I'm reading about. Peter Mayle's books on Provence made me hungry for eggplants and garlic. I drink a lot of tea and munch scones when I read Agatha Christie. And when I was reading *Clan of the Cave Bear*, I kept wanting to forage outside for stuff." (Unfortunately, she lived in lower Manhattan at the time.)

Another friend was inspired to take a class in Chinese cooking after she read *The Kitchen God's Wife*, by Amy Tan; another went on a Mexican food kick while reading Laura Esquivel's *Like Water for Chocolate*. Colette's books always make me want café au lait and crusty French bread. Visit a library; see what whets; see what whets *your* appetite.

One more suggestion: Try listening to appropriate music while you cook. I sometimes like to play Italian opera when I'm making pasta, for instance—it helps to get me in the mood. Cajun food and Cajun music are a natural match. Edith Piaf is great for French food. Experiment.

Cooking in sync with your body cycles and moods: Many of us find that our feelings about food change with our hormonal tides. I feel more like cooking when I'm premenstrual than any other time in my cycle—so I cook extra on those days and freeze some to save for ovulation, when I'd rather be doing other things instead. On the days when I feel especially mentally alert, I make up menus and shopping lists. If I'm in a sociable phase, I have friends over for potlucks or community cooks. When I'm feeling more hermitlike (especially in winter), I do lots of baking and take that quiet time to write or dream. When we pay attention to our moods and honor them in the kitchen, we honor ourselves. Honor what you're feeling today.

Supplies

*I*t isn't always possible to get what you need locally. If you can't find mugwort or goddess statues anywhere nearby, try these mail-order suppliers—they offer inspiration as well as the things you need. Call or write for catalogs, some of which are beautiful enough to frame, or visit their Web sites.

Cooking Gadgets

Gooseberry Patch
P.O. Box 190
Delaware, OH 43015
(800) 854-6673
www.gooseberry.com

(It has great cookie-cutters—including leaf-shaped ones—egg-shaped soaps, and an appreciation of the seasons.)

Williams-Sonoma
P.O. Box 7456
San Francisco, CA 94120-7456
(877) 812-6235
www.williams-sonoma.com

Earth-Conscious Home Products

Real Goods
360 Interlocken Boulevard
Broomfield, CO 80021-3440
(800) 994-4243
www.realgoods.com

Harmony
360 Interlocken Boulevard
Suite 300
Broomfield, CO 80021
(800) 869-3446
www.gaiam.com

Seventh Generation
212 Battery Street, Suite A
Burlington, VT 05401-5281
(802) 658-3773
www.seventhgen.com

(The above three companies sell all-natural cleaning products, recycled papers, natural fabrics, and much more.)

Witch Wonders and Goddess Goodies

Archie McPhee
P.O. Box 30852
Seattle, WA 98103
(206) 745-0711
www.halcyon.com.mcphee

(This is not goddess- or witch-oriented, but is such a terrific source for chili-pepper lights, wonderfully gaudy Protection Packets, and a refreshing sense of humor.)

M'Lou Brubaker
14015 W. Co Road 578
Goodland, MN 55742
(218) 492-4487
www.craftswomen.com/m'louBrubaker

(jewelry)

Kate Cartwright
Box 824
Ketchum, ID 83340
www.katecartwright.com

(rubber stamps; send $1 for catalog)

The Dreaming Goddess
9 Collegeview Avenue
Poughkeepsie, NY 12603
(845) 473-2206
www.dreaminggoddess.com

(an incredible selection of tarot decks, women's spirituality books, jewelry, crystals, statues, Native Americana—it's all there)

Jane Iris Designs, Inc.
P.O. Box 608
Graton, CA 95444
(800) 828-5687

(jewelry)

Pyramid Books
P.O. Box 3333, Altid Park
Chelmsford, MA 01824-0933
(800) 333-4220
www.pyramidcollection.com

(meditation tools, books, candles, tapes)

Sacred Source
Box WW
Crozet, VA 22932-0163
(800) 290-6203
www.sacredsource.com

(drums, books, prints, statues)

Herbs

Blessed Herbs
109 Barre Plains Road
Oakham, MA 01068
(800) 489-4372
www.blessedherbs.com

(organic and wildcrafted herbs and
liquid extracts)

Frontier Natural Products Co-op
P.O. Box 299
Norway, IA 52318
www.frontiercoop.com

Jean's Greens
119 Sulphur Spring Road
Norway, NY 13416
(315) 845-6500
www.jeansgreens.com

Mountain Rose Herbs
20818 High Street
North San Juan, CA 95960
(800) 879-3337
www.mountainroseherbs.com

Suggested Reading

*T*he *following lists are* good jumping-off places for your own explorations into green housekeeping, the Goddess, earth-centered spirituality, herbs, aromatherapy, rituals, and other delights. Many of these selections include detailed bibliographies that will lead you deeper. Trust your own ability to find what you need.

Aromatherapy

Berwick, Ann. *Holistic Aromatherapy: Balance the Body and Soul with Essential Oils*. St. Paul, Minn.: Llewellyn, 1994.

Cunningham, Scott. *The Complete Book of Incense, Oils and Brews*. St. Paul, Minn.: Llewellyn, 1992.

Davis, Patricia. *Aromatherapy A–Z*. Great Britain: C. W. Daniel, 1988.

Dye, Jane. *Aromatherapy for Women and Children*. Great Britain: C. W. Daniel, 1992.

Tisserand, Maggie. *Aromatherapy for Women*. Rochester, Vt.: Healing Arts Press, 1988.

Cookbooks, Books about Cooking and Food

Alper, Nicole, and Lynette Rohrer. *Wild Women in the Kitchen: 101 Rambunctious Recipes and 99 Tasty Tales*. Berkeley, Calif.: Conari Press, 1996.

Callan, Ginny. *Horn of the Moon Cookbook*. New York: Harper and Row, 1987.

_____. *Beyond the Moon Cookbook*. New York: HarperCollins, 1996.

Colwin, Laurie. *Home Cooking: A Writer in the Kitchen*. New York: HarperCollins, 1988.

David, Marc. *Nourishing Wisdom: A Mind-Body Approach to Nutrition and Well-Being*. New York: Crown, 1991.

d'Avila-Latourrette, Brother Victor-Antoine. *This Good Food: Contemporary French Vegetarian Recipes from a Monastery Kitchen*. Woodstock, N.Y.: Overlook Press, 1993.

Hurd, Frank J., and Rosalie Hurd. *Ten Talents Cookbook*. Collegedale, Tenn.: The College Press, 1968.

Katzen, Mollie. *The Enchanted Broccoli Forest*. Berkeley, Calif.: Ten Speed Press, 1982.

_____. *Moosewood Cookbook*. Berkeley, Calif.: Ten Speed Press, 1977.

_____. *Still Life with Menu Cookbook*. Berkeley, Calif.: Ten Speed Press, 1994.

Lair, Cynthia. *Feeding the Whole Family: Down-to-Earth Cookbook and Whole Foods Guide*. San Diego: LuraMedia, 1994.

Nearing, Helen. *Simple Food for the Good Life*. Walepole, N.H.: Stillpoint Publishing, 1985.

Robertson, Laurel, Carol Flinders, and Brian Ruppenthal. *Laurel's Kitchen Recipes*. Berkeley, Calif.: Ten Speed Press, 1993.

_____. *The New Laurel's Kitchen: A Handbook for Vegetarian Cookery and Nutrition*. Berkeley, Calif.: Ten Speed Press, 1976.

Rombauer, Irma, and Marion Rombauer Becker. *Joy of Cooking*. New York: Penguin, 1973.

Shaw, Maura D., and Sydna Altschuler Byrne. *Foods from Mother Earth: A Basic Cookbook for Young Vegetarians (and Anybody Else)*. Wappingers Falls, N.Y.: Shawangunk Press, 1994.

Thomas, Anna. *The Vegetarian Epicure*. New York: Random House, 1972.

_____. *The Vegetarian Epicure, Book Two*. New York: Alfred A. Knopf, 1978.

_____. *The New Vegetarian Epicure*. New York: Alfred A. Knopf, 1996.

Vitell, Bettina. *A Taste of Heaven and Earth*. New York: HarperCollins, 1993.

Waters, Alice. *Chez Panisse Vegetables*. New York: HarperCollins, 1996.

_____. *Fanny at Chez Panisse*. New York: HarperCollins, 1992.

Divination Tools

These are my personal favorites, including decks I usually recommend to people who are just beginning their tarot explorations.

Carr-Gomm, Philip, and Stephanie Carr-Gomm. *The Druid Animal Oracle*. New York: Simon and Schuster, 1994.

Jackson, Nigel, and Silver Ravenwolf. *The Rune Mysteries*. St. Paul, Minn.: Llewellyn, 1996.

Matthews, Caitlín. *Celtic Wisdom Tarot*. Rochester, Vt.: Destiny Books, 1999.

Smith, Pamela Colman, and Arthur Edward Waite. *Rider-Waite Tarot*. Stamford, Conn.: U.S. Games, 1995.

Vogel, Karen, and Vicki Noble. *Motherpeace Tarot: Deck and Book Set*. Stamford, Conn.: U.S. Games, 1997.

Earth-Centered Spirituality, the Goddess, and Ritual

Beck, Renee, and Sydney Barbara Metrick. *The Art of Ritual*. Berkeley, Calif.: Celestial Arts, 1990.

Blair, Nancy. *Amulets of the Goddess*. Oakland, Calif.: Wingbow Press, 1993.

Bolen, Jean Shinoda. *Goddesses in Everywoman: A New Psychology of Women*. New York: Harper and Row, 1984.

Bowes, Sue. *Woman's Magic: Rituals, Meditations and Magical Ways*. York Beach, Maine: Weiser Books, 1999.

Budapest, Z. *Grandmother Moon: Lunar Magic in Our Lives*. San Francisco: HarperSanFrancisco, 1991.

_____. *The Goddess in the Office*. San Francisco: HarperSanFrancisco, 1993.

_____. *The Grandmother of Time*. San Francisco: HarperSanFrancisco, 1989.

_____. *The Holy Book of Women's Mysteries*, vols. 1 and 2. Berkeley, Calif.: Wingbow Press, 1986 rev.

Cahill, Sedonia, and Joshua Halpern. *Ceremonial Circle: Practice, Ritual, and Renewal for Personal and Community Healing*. San Francisco: HarperSanFrancisco, 1992.

Campanelli, Pauline. *Ancient Ways: Reclaiming Pagan Traditions*. St. Paul, Minn.: Llewellyn, 1991.

_____. *Wheel of the Year: Living the Magickal Life*. St. Paul, Minn.: Llewellyn, 1987.

Carr-Gomm, Philip, and Stephanie Carr-Gomm. *The Druid Animal Oracle: Working with the Sacred Animals of Druid Tradition*. New York: Simon and Schuster, 1994.

Curott, Phyllis. *Book of Shadows: A Modern Woman's Journey into the Wisdom of Witchcraft and the Magic of the Goddess*. New York: Broadway Books, 1998.

Duerk, Judith. *Circle of Stones*. San Diego: LuraMedia, 1989.

Edwards, Carolyn McVickar. *The Storyteller's Goddess: Tales of the Goddess and Her Wisdom from Around the World*. New York: HarperCollins, 1991.

Eisler, Riane. *The Chalice and the Blade: Our History, Our Future*. San Francisco: HarperSanFrancisco, 1986.

Gimbutas, Marija. *The Language of the Goddess*. San Francisco: HarperSanFrancisco, 1989.

Johnson, Cait, and Maura D. Shaw. *Celebrating the Great Mother: A Handbook of Earth-Honoring Activities for Parents and Children*. Rochester, Vt.: Destiny Books, 1995.

Monaghan, Patricia. *The Book of Goddesses and Heroines*. New York: E. P. Dutton, 1981.

_____. *The Goddess Path: Myths, Invocations and Rituals*. St. Paul, Minn.: Llewellyn, 1999.

Nahmad, Claire. *Earth Magic: A Wisewoman's Guide to Herbal, Astrological, and Other Folk Wisdom*. Rochester, Vt.: Destiny Books, 1994.

Noble, Vicki. *Motherpeace: A Way to the Goddess through Myth, Art and Tarot*. San Francisco: Harper and Row, 1983.

_____. *Shakti Woman: Feeling Our Fire, Healing Our World*. San Francisco: HarperSanFrancisco, 1991.

Sjöö, Monica, and Barbara Mor. *The Great Cosmic Mother: Rediscovering the Religion of the Earth*. San Francisco: HarperSanFrancisco, 1987.

Starck, Marcia. *Women's Medicine Ways: Cross-Cultural Rites of Passage*. Freedom, Calif.: Crossing Press, 1993.

Starhawk. *The Spiral Dance: A Rebirth of the Ancient Religion of the Great Goddess—Rituals, Invocations, Exercises, Magic*. San Francisco: Harper and Row, 1999.

Starhawk and Hilary Valentine. *The Twelve Wild Swans: A Journey to the Realm of Magic, Healing and Action*. San Francisco: HarperSanFrancisco, 2000.

Stein, Diane. *The Women's Spirituality Book.* St. Paul, Minn.: Llewellyn, 1998.

Stone, Merlin. *Ancient Mirrors of Womanhood: Our Goddess and Heroine Heritage.* New York: New Sibylline, 1979.

_____. *When God Was a Woman.* New York: Harcourt Brace Jovanovich, 1978.

Swain, Sally. *Oh My Goddess!* New York: Penguin, 1994.

Teish, Luisa. *Jambalaya: The Natural Woman's Book of Personal Charms and Practical Rituals.* San Francisco: Harper and Row, 1985.

Waldherr, Kris. *The Book of Goddesses.* Hillsboro, Ore.: Beyond Words Publishing, 1995.

Walker, Barbara G. *The Crone.* San Francisco: Harper and Row, 1985.

_____. *The Woman's Dictionary of Symbols and Sacred Objects.* San Francisco: HarperSanFrancisco, 1988.

_____. *The Woman's Encyclopedia of Myths and Secrets.* San Francisco: Harper and Row, 1983.

_____. *Women's Rituals.* San Francisco: Harper and Row, 1990.

Weinstein, Marion. *Earth Magic: A Dianic Book of Shadows.* Custer, Wash.: Phoenix, 1986.

Wilshire, Donna. *Virgin Mother Crone: Myths and Mysteries of the Triple Goddess.* Rochester, Vt.: Inner Traditions, 1994.

Worth, Valerie. *The Crone's Book of Words.* St. Paul, Minn.: Llewellyn , 1986.

Food for Thought

These are a few of my touchstones—books that, although they don't exactly fit into any of the other categories in this suggested list, have had a positive impact on my life. One common thread that connects these very different authors is a deep appreciation of women and the Earth, and an awareness of the sacred in the everyday. While our culture conspires to put our spirits to sleep, these will wake you up. You may find, after sampling a few of these offerings, that you are inspired to begin a list of your own. Share it with your friends!

Ackerman, Diane. *A Natural History of the Senses.* New York: Random House, 1990.

Bender, Sue. *Everyday Sacred: A Woman's Journey Home.* New York: HarperCollins, 1995.

_____. *Plain and Simple: A Woman's Journey to the Amish*. New York: HarperCollins, 1989.

Cameron, Julia. *The Artist's Way: A Spiritual Path to Higher Creativity*. New York: Putnam, 1992.

Colette. Any of her novels; even her biographies are delicious—this woman had a real passion for life and for good food.

Cunningham, Elizabeth. *Daughter of the Shining Isles*. Barrytown, N.Y.: Station Hill Press, 2000.

_____. *The Return of the Goddess*. Barrytown, N.Y.: Station Hill Press, 1992.

Estes, Clarissa Pinkola. *Women Who Run with the Wolves: Myths and Stories of the Wild Woman Archetype*. New York: Ballantine, 1992.

Fisher, M. F. K. Anything you can find of hers is valuable, but *The Art of Eating* is especially wonderful.

Linthwaite, Illona, ed. *Ain't I a Woman! A Book of Women's Poetry from Around the World*. New York: Random House, 1993.

Louden, Jennifer. *The Woman's Comfort Book: A Self-Nurturing Guide for Restoring Balance in Your Life*. San Francisco: HarperSanFrancisco, 1992.

Martz, Sandra, ed. *When I Am an Old Woman, I Shall Wear Purple*. Watsonville, Calif.: Papier-Mâché Press, 1987.

Perkins, John. *The World Is As You Dream It: Shamanic Teachings from the Amazon and Andes*. Rochester, Vt.: Inner Traditions, 1994.

Sarton, May. Any of the journals, but especially *Journal of a Solitude* and *Plant Dreaming Deep*.

Scott, Anne. *Serving Fire: Food for Thought, Body, and Soul*. Berkeley, Calif.: Celestial Arts, 1994.

Williams, Terry Tempest. *An Unspoken Hunger*. New York: Random House, 1994.

Green Housekeeping

Berthold-Bond, Annie. *Clean and Green: The Complete Guide to Nontoxic and Environmentally Safe Housekeeping*. Woodstock, N.Y.: Ceres Press, 1990.

Berthold-Bond, Annie, and Mothers and Others. *The Green Kitchen Handbook*. New York: HarperCollins, 1997.

Dadd, Debra Lynn. *The Nontoxic Home: Protecting Yourself and Your Family from Everyday Toxics and Health Hazards*. Los Angeles: Jeremy P. Tarcher, 1986.

_____. *Nontoxic, Natural, and Earthwise: How to Protect Yourself and Your Family from Harmful Products and Live in Harmony with the Earth*. Los Angeles: Jeremy P. Tarcher, 1990.

_____. *Sustaining the Earth: Choosing Consumer Products That Are Safe for You, Your Family, and the Earth*. Los Angeles: Jeremy P. Tarcher, 1994.

Herbs, Magical Foods, Wild Foods

Berneth, Stefen. *Common Weeds*. Mineola, N.Y.: Dover, 1976.

Beyerl, Paul. *The Master Book of Herbalism*. Custer, Wash.: Phoenix, 1984.

Cunningham, Scott. *Cunningham's Encyclopedia of Magical Herbs*. St. Paul, Minn.: Llewellyn, 1985.

_____. *Magical Herbalism*. St. Paul, Minn.: Llewellyn, 1983.

_____. *The Magic in Food*. St. Paul, Minn.: Llewellyn, 1991.

Griggs, Barbara. *The Green Witch Herbal: Restoring Nature's Magic in Home, Health, and Beauty Care*. Rochester, Vt.: Inner Traditions, 1994.

Mabey, Richard, ed. *The New Age Herbal*. New York: Macmillan, 1988.

Shanberg, Karen, and Stan Tekiela. *Plantworks: Field Guide, Recipes, Activities*. Cambridge, Minn.: Adventure, 1991.

Weed, Susun. *Healing Wise*. Woodstock, N.Y.: Ash Tree Publishing, 1989.

Meditation, Mindfulness, Spiritual Practice

Ban Breathnach, Sarah. *Simple Abundance: A Daybook of Comfort and Joy*. New York: Warner Books, 1995.

Chodron, Pema. *When Things Fall Apart*. Boston: Shambhala, 2000.

Cowan, Tom. *Shamanism as a Spiritual Practice for Daily Life*. Freedom, Calif.: Crossing Press, 1996.

Gawain, Shakti. *Creative Visualization*. Mill Valley, Calif.: Whatever Publishing, 1978.

Hanh, Thich Nhat. *The Miracle of Mindfulness: A Manual on Meditation*. Boston: Beacon Press, 1987.

Mariechild, Diane. *Mother Wit: A Guide to Healing and Psychic Development*. Freedom, Calif.: Crossing Press, 1988.

_____. *Open Mind: Women's Daily Inspiration for Becoming Mindful*. San Francisco: HarperSanFrancisco, 1995.

Moore, Thomas. *Care of the Soul: A Guide for Cultivating Depth and Sacredness in Everyday Life*. New York: HarperCollins, 1992.

Native American Issues

Brave Bird, Mary, with Richard Erdoes. *Ohitika Woman*. New York: Grove Press, 1993.

Brown, Dee. *Bury My Heart at Wounded Knee*. New York: Holt, Rinehart, Winston, 1970.

Crow Dog, Mary. *Lakota Woman*. New York: HarperCollins, 1990.

Farley, Ronnie. *Women of the Native Struggle: Portraits and Testimony of Native American Women*. New York: Orion, 1993.

Matthiessen, Peter. *In the Spirit of Crazy Horse*. New York: Penguin, 1992.

Publications

The Beltane Papers: A Journal of Women's Mysteries, P.O. Box 29694, Bellingham, WA 98228-1694. Phone: (360) 647-1264. members.xoom.com/TBP_Magazine

Circle Magazine: Celebrating Nature, Spirit, and Magic, P.O. Box 219, Mt. Horeb, WI 53572-0219. Phone: (608) 924-2216. circle@mhtc.net or www.circlesanctuary.org

SageWoman: Celebrating the Goddess in Every Woman, P.O. Box 641, Point Arena, CA 95468-0641. Phone: (888) 724-3966. www.sagewoman.com.

Index

BOOKS OF RELATED INTEREST

A DRUID'S HERBAL FOR THE SACRED EARTH YEAR
by Ellen Evert Hopman

BEING A PAGAN
Druids, Wiccans, and Witches Today
by Ellen Evert Hopman

THE PAGAN BOOK OF DAYS
A Guide to the Festivals, Traditions, and Sacred Days of the Year
by Nigel Pennick

THE PAGAN MYSTERIES OF HALLOWEEN
Celebrating the Dark Half of the Year
by Jean Markale

WOMEN OF THE CELTS
by Jean Markale

TRADITIONAL FOODS ARE YOUR BEST MEDICINE
Improving Health and Longevity with Native Nutrition
by Ronald F. Schmid, N.D.

THE SEASONAL DETOX DIET
Using Food and Fasting throughout the Year to Rejuvenate Body and Spirit
by Carrie L'Esperance

THE HEMP COOKBOOK
From Seed to Shining Seed
by Todd Dalotto

Inner Traditions • Bear & Company
P.O. Box 388 • Rochester, VT 05767
1-800-246-8648 • www.InnerTraditions.com

Or contact your local bookseller